The Technique of
Freeform Design

Nancy M. Searles

Order from:
Weaver's Way
P.O. Box 70
Columbus, North Carolina 28722

ISBN 0-9613894-0-0

First Printing - May, 1984
Second Printing - May, 1990

All photgraphs are by the author unless otherwise stated.

Printed by:
Home Mountain Publishing Co., Inc.
Valparaiso, Indiana 46383

This book is dedicated to my mother, Elberta Hubbard Marsh, who taught with love and patience.

"Art is beauty, and beauty is a gratification, a peace and a solace to every normal man and woman. Beautiful sounds, beautiful colors, beautiful proportions, beautiful thoughts — how our souls hunger for them! . . . Art is the expression of man's joy in his work. You must let the man work with hand and brain, and then out of the joy of this marriage, beauty will be born. And the beauty mirrors the best in the soul of man — it shows the spirit of God that runs through him."
Elbert Hubbard

Elbert Hubbard, whose quotes appear throughout the book, is the author's great-grandfather and is, himself, an author.

Acknowledgements

The writing and publishing of a book may be considered the sole effort of the author. Nothing could be farther from the truth!—I owe a great deal to the following who willingly gave of their time and talents:

Editors: Teri and Jack Baker, Ann Christensen, Denna Gleason, Kathy O'Neal, and Lu Terock;

Proofreaders: Betsy Lepel and Deb Macke;

Weavers who learned the techniques and wove specific pieces: Ann Christensen, Doris Cox, Lois Crocker, Nancy Eversole, Betty Johannesen, Nancy Keegstra, Elaine Lee, Betsy Lepel, Deb Macke, Jo Ann Nelson, Mugs O'Toole, Mimi Pope, Linda Rockwell, Kathie Roig, Pat Short;

Contributors of individual freeform pieces: Jim Ahrens, Birgit Barron, Paula Blaski, Marcy Boettcher, Agnes Galik, Freddie Ingebrigtsen, Susan Koski, Peggy MacArthur, Mae Matousek, Sally Meyer, Lynn Moore, Bev Mousseau, Joan Wells, Dian Zahner;

Cover piece: Kathie Roig

Graphics: Linda Howson

Graphs: Nancy G. B. Roberts

Preface sketch: Ken Saathoff

Design for the shuttles which appears throughout the book: Paula Krause

Special thanks to the following for efforts beyond...:

Elaine Lee who wove the pieces used at the beginning of each Chapter and in Contents;

Doris Cox who developed freeform overshot;

Nancy G. B. Roberts for her help during the final weeks of publication;

my patient family!

Acknowledgements are given to:

Ahrens & Violette Looms, Inc. for permission to use a photograph of an AVL loom and dobby head;

Boris Kroll Fabrics, Inc. for permission to use photographs of their Jacquard loom and fabrics;

LeClerc Corporation for permission to use a photograph of a LeClerc shuttle (page 25);

Museum of Science and Industry, Chicago, for permission to use photographs taken at the exhibit "China, 7000 years of Discovery";

Arthur W. Olson for designing the handcrafted freeform shuttle shown on page 25.

Contents

INSIGHTS - The listing in Contents includes only the general topics involving information not directly related to the Chapter content.

Preface

"There is nothing new under the sun" is a statement as applicable to weaving as it is to all artforms. Most basic techniques we use today have been in existence for several thousand years, but the way in which each of us combines and interprets these techniques results in self-expression—in creativity.

The concept of freeform design involves bending the lines of traditional block weaves so that a 2-dimensional design of any shape may be created wherever desired in the piece. The look of the traditional weave (its weave structure) is retained, but the weaver is able to free himself from the vertical and horizontal lines established by the threading and treadling of traditional block weaves.

At this point you probably wish to tell me that the idea is an old one indeed, and that the draw loom has accomplished this very thing for the past 5 centuries or so, as has the use of the pick-up stick. You are correct on both counts. But my desire has been to develop a method of freeform design for the four-harness loom which involves no draw system or pick-up stick.

I was fortunate to have this desire fulfilled in a workshop devoted to learning damask woven on a 4-harness loom with no pick-up system. Learning damask as a four-harness freeform design technique should perhaps have satisfied my quest. But instead, it brought to my mind another question. The process of answering this question has led to several years of research, the beginning of teaching and sharing the results of my research and, finally, this book.

The question was this: Since damask was originally a block weave and can now be woven successfully as a four-harness freeform design technique, would it be possible to convert other block weaves

in the same manner so that they, too, could be woven in freeform design? The question was, even at the time I posed it, rhetorical. I was certain that the process that worked for converting damask would also work when used with other block weaves. It is this process, as well as the weaves resulting from the process, that will be shared.

Many of the pieces in this book have been woven by individuals who take their weaving very seriously, but consider it to be a pastime rather than a profession. There are several valuable contributions from weavers with less than one year of experience, and most have been weaving for fewer than five years. The material presented is for the intermediate to advanced weaver who wishes a new creative approach to weaving and an enjoyable challenge. However, enough guidelines and hints are given that a newer weaver should be able to use the techniques with confidence. The creative process need not be threatening. We all do possess creative ability, although the process may come more easily to some than others. Let your personal creativity blossom with the help of these techniques!

With instructions and project ideas as starting points, I am confident that you will be comfortable with a new approach to block weaves. After some experimentation, perhaps you will even ask yourself "I wonder what would happen if. . .". And by allowing your creativity to address that question, you may discover another technique or variation.

We may think there is nothing new under the sun, but thank heaven each of us can view the horizon differently!

NMS March, 1984.

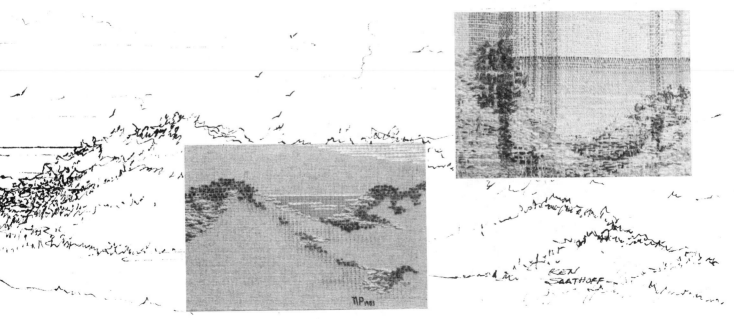

Heritage

The Draw Loom, Jacquard, Damask, & Brocade

The Early Treadle Loom

The first evidence of the treadle loom dates to the Han dynasty in China some 2000 years before the Christian Era. The loom was very simply constructed, consisting of a two-shed mechanism with one or two treadles. Although this loom was designed for weaving plain weave, it was possible to alter the length of weft floats by permitting the weft to pass over several warp ends instead of one. The result was a form of damask called "Han damask". It was also possible to embellish a plain weave fabric by brocading—adding weft yarns in addition to the ground weft which appeared on the fabric surface in designated areas.

Development of The Draw Loom

With the advent of the draw loom, weaving damask and brocade was simplified. Warp ends could be raised individually in addition to being part of a ground plain weave, which made it possible to weave damask and brocade more quickly than by any other method used prior to that time.

The draw loom was probably developed in Iran. Discoveries of intricately patterned fabrics involving evenly spaced pattern repeats attest to this. While authorities place its development somewhere between the 3rd and 7th Centuries A.D. during the Sassanian Dynasty, a one-man draw loom from China is shown in *Photo I-1* which is thought to have been in use several centuries prior to the Christian Era.

Ph. I-1. An ancient one-man draw loom used in China, possibly as long ago as five thousand years.

Weaving on the draw loom was found to be more efficient if one person wove and a second person pulled the drawcords into position for the pattern rows. It is this two-man draw loom with at least one draw boy assisting the weaver which has remained the preferred method of operation.

In China, the one-man draw loom was followed some two thousand years ago by the more familiar two-man draw loom. This loom remains in use today for the weaving of intricately patterned brocade and damask fabrics. Those who weave on draw looms in China apprentice for a number of years to learn the intricacies of the weave system, and develop the timing necessary to co-ordinate the efforts of the weaver and draw boy. The two-man draw loom used in China today is shown with the brocade fabric typically woven.

Ph. I-2. Two-man draw loom used in China today.

Ph. I-3. The drawcords, through which the warp ends are threaded, are pulled, lifting individual warp ends to create a shed for pattern development.

Ph. I-4. The draw boy pulling the appropriate drawcords to create a shed.

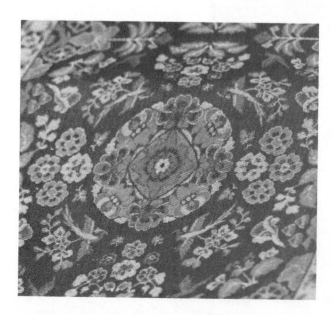

Ph. I-5. The six-harness brocade material being woven on the Chinese two-man draw loom.

The use of the two-man draw loom spread to Europe by the 12th Century A.D. It was used widely in Italy by the 14th Century and was in equal demand in France by the 17th Century. In both countries, the draw loom was used primarily for the weaving of elaborate damasks, brocades and velvets. The fabrics shown in *Photos I-6* and *I-7* are typical of those woven in Italy in the 1400s and later.

Ph. I-6. Italian silk fabric woven with the Chinese phoenix design. 15th Century. Photo courtesy of Lisa Peterson.

Ph. I-7. Italian brocade fabric. 18th Century.

The draw loom has withstood the test of time because it permits the weaving of complex weave structures in a straightforward manner. One serious difficulty exists with the draw loom, however, other than the time necessary for preparation, size of the loom, and number of weavers necessary to operate it. When a draw threading is prepared for a particular pattern, that is the only pattern which can be woven. In order to change a pattern, the entire lengthy process of preparation must be repeated.

The Jacquard Loom

In 1803, Joseph Marie Jacquard developed a draw loom in France which accommodates all of the weaves of the draw loom and permits the weaving of many different patterns with one preparation of the warp and loom. With the Jacquard loom, the necessity of a draw boy is eliminated.

Cards are punched, tied together, and placed at the side of the loom in a continuous loop. The card at the top of the loop is positioned over "pins", each of which is connected to an individual heddle or group of heddles. The holes in each card let only certain pins through, raising only these warp ends to form a pattern shed. When the shuttle has passed through that shed, the cards are moved and the next card is positioned at the top of the loop. To weave a different pattern, the set of cards is changed. *Photos I-8 and I-9* show a typical Jacquard loom of the late 1800s and a set of cards, laced and ready for use.

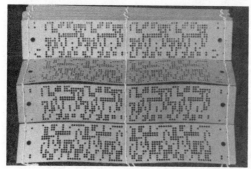

Ph. I-8. Jacquard loom, circa 1870 (above).

Ph. I-9. Cards for the Jacquard loom which have been punched and laced, and are ready to be positioned on the loom (left).

The Jacquard loom, like the draw loom, involves time-consuming preparation. The process of drawing the pattern, punching and lacing the cards together can take several weeks. However, the weaving process is faster than the draw loom. And with the other advantages taken into account, the development of the Jacquard loom was a definite step forward.

The Jacquard loom was introduced to the American textile industry early in the 1800s and has been used since that time. The Jacquard is used extensively today for industrial weaving of clothing and upholstery fabrics in Europe as well as in this Country. *Photos I-10* and *I-11* are of fabrics woven on today's Jacquard looms at Boris Kroll Fabrics, Inc. in New York and the industrial Jacquard loom on which the fabrics are woven.

Ph. I-10. The draw system and cards of today's industrial Jacquard loom. Photo courtesy of Lisa Peterson.

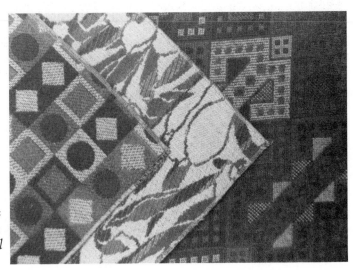

Ph. I-11. Fabrics typically woven on the industrial Jacquard loom.

Computers and the Dobby Head

Many of the industrial Jacquard looms today are operated by cards which have been punched by computer. It is logical to involve the computer, since the original concept of using cards for the Jacquard loom is, in itself, the forerunner of computer "on" and "off" binary vocabulary. When applied to the Jacquard loom, this binary system means that there either *is* a hole in the card through which the pin passes ("on"), or there is *not* ("off"). The use of the computer greatly reduces the time necessary to prepare the design and the cards.

The development of the draw loom and Jacquard apply primarily to industrial weaving. Neither process is reasonable for the average weaver who produces limited yards of fabric and changes projects frequently.

An attachment is available for several smaller looms used by the home weaver called a "dobby head". The pegging system for the dobby head allows multiple-harness weaves to be woven without the difficulties of treadling multiple-harness tie-ups. This is a definite advancement in the ease with which complex weaves can be woven.

A number of loom manufacturers are now also able to equip looms with devices which are compatible with home computers. While these devices, both dobby head and computer, do afford the weaver access to an increased number of treadling possibilities, it is not as yet reasonable to weave two-dimensional designs in freeform design technique. The number of "cards" necessary to weave in the style of the Jacquard loom is simply too great.

Ph. I-12. A bar of the AVL loom pegging system being placed in position by Jim Ahrens, one of the developers of the loom. Photo courtesy of Ahrens & Violette Looms, Inc.

Freeform Design Technique

My research efforts are devoted to bringing the facilities of the draw loom and the Jacquard to the weaver who works at home with a four-harness loom. Preparation time for weaving a design in what I call "freeform design technique" is no more extensive than what is necessary to warp and thread a loom for most projects. The additional time comes with the weaving. The shuttle is not thrown selvedge-to-selvedge in the traditional manner, but is moved across the row somewhat differently, changing the treadling as the shuttle advances. With freeform design technique, as with the draw loom and the Jacquard, the results render the efforts worthwhile!

In addition to the more commonly woven damask and brocades, I have developed methods for weaving 14 freeform designs derived from traditional four-harness weaves. The design possibility using these techniques is virtually unlimited! Photographs show the wide variety of techniques to be presented in this book. These photographs are used to identify each technique in the Table of Contents and at the beginning of each Chapter. Presenting them together provides an overview of the possibilities inherent in freeform design technique.

Freeform Design Technique
Pieces Woven by Elaine Lee.

Freeform twill (left).
Weft inlay added to freeform twill (below).

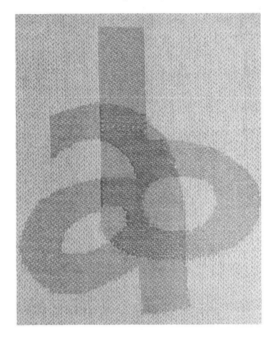

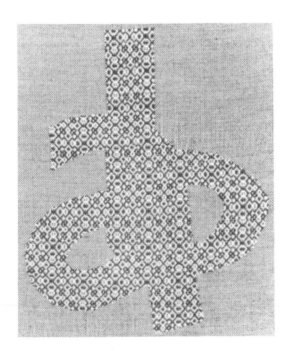

Freeform overshot (above).
Freeform Summer & Winter woven with a single repeat (right).

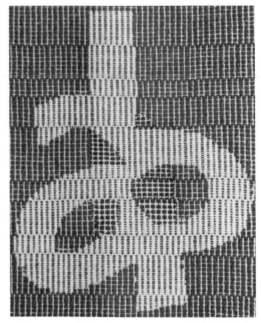

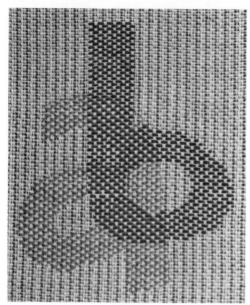

Freeform Ms & Os woven with
two pattern wefts.

Freeform huck.

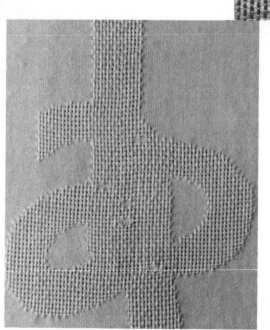

Freeform bronson lace.

Freeform lace huck (left).
Brocade (below).

Double weft twill (left).
Double weft Ms & Os (below).

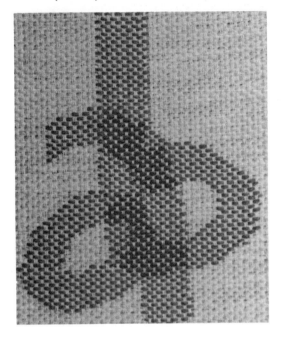

Double weft Marsh (above).
Double weft Summer & Winter (right).

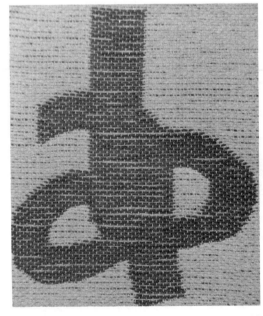

Broadweft Summer & Winter (right).
Broadweft Ms & Os (below).

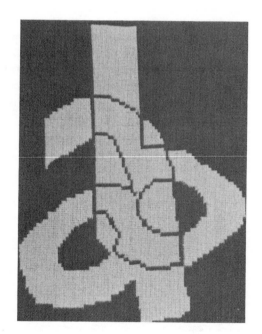

Freeform double weave (above).
Freeform Finnweave (left).

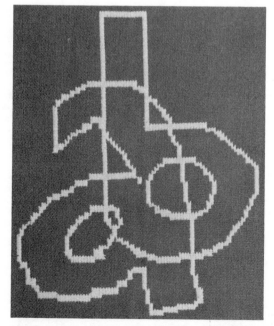

Section I

Nine freeform design techniques are presented in Section I. The weave structures involved in the techniques are derivatives of traditional 4-harness block weaves, and, in most cases, the weave structures of the traditional weaves are recognizable in the freeform design techniques.

These techniques all result in fabrics which are light to medium weight. The warps for these weaves are sett to square, as they would be for the traditional weaves. Weft yarns are also, for the most part, those which are used for the traditional weaves.

Freeform design techniques presented in Section I include twill, overshot, Summer & Winter, Ms & Os, huck, lace huck, bronson lace, and brocade.

Selected Glossary

The following terminology is essential to the understanding of the techniques presented and the method of weaving. The terms are also included in the Glossary.

WEAVE STRUCTURE

THE PARTICULAR WAY IN WHICH WARP AND WEFT INTERACT TO FORM A SPECIFIC INTERLACEMENT.

RISING SHED

All draw-downs in this book relate to the rising shed loom, on which the *HARNESSES ARE LIFTED WHEN ACTIVATED.* The use of an "o" for the tie-ups in the draw-downs indicates a rising shed.

HARNESS COMBINATION

THE HARNESSES LIFTED AT ONE TIME TO FORM A SHED ON A RISING SHED LOOM. The term "harness combination" is synonymous with the term "tie-up" with which you may be more familiar. However, because the term "tie-up" has several different meanings in American weaving terminology, it will be used only in the draw-down (see the definition of "tie-ups" below).

TIE-UPS

THAT PART OF THE DRAW-DOWN INDICATING WHICH HARNESS IS TIED TO WHICH TREADLE. Figure A details a draw-down of a warp-faced twill with direct tie-ups. *Figure B* details the same warp-faced twill in a draw-down with multiple tie-ups. Both tie-ups are for the rising shed loom.

Fig. A. Warp-faced twill with direct tie-ups.

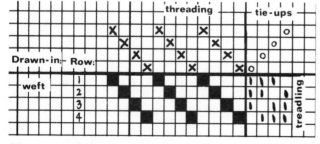

Fig. B. Warp-faced twill with multiple tie-ups.

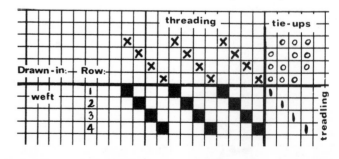

DIRECT TIE-UPS

EACH TREADLE ON A FLOOR LOOM, OR LEVER ON A TABLE LOOM, IS TIED TO ONLY ONE HARNESS. Therefore, with four harnesses, there are four treadles or levers in use, one tied to each harness. All draw-downs in this book show direct tie-ups, and if more than one harness is to be activated to form a shed, there is a mark under each of the harnesses to be activated for that row.

MULTIPLE TIE-UPS

EACH TREADLE ON A FLOOR LOOM IS TIED TO A HARNESS COMBINATION. If you have a floor loom with six treadles, then you may wish to tie one harness combination to one treadle instead of having to activate each harness separately as with direct tie-ups. All of the freeform weaves discussed, except one, require six or fewer harness combinations and can, therefore, be woven with each harness combination tied to a treadle. The exception is freeform twill which has eight harness combinations and which must, therefore, be woven using direct tie-ups.

TO TREADLE

TO ACTIVATE A HARNESS COMBINATION.

TREADLING SEQUENCE

A PARTICULAR ORDER IN WHICH THE HARNESS COMBINATIONS ARE LIFTED.

1.

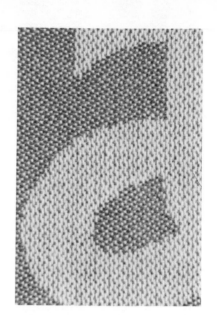

Freeform Twill

Freeform Design Technique Defined

Freeform design technique is defined by this author as: A weave system comprised of one threading sequence which is repeated selvedge-to-selvedge, and which can be treadled to produce at least two different weave structures by using separate harness combinations for each of the weaves. Each row consists of two harness combinations, one for each weave structure. The treadling within each row is alternated between these two harness combinations to produce the two weaves in different areas of the piece.

Introduction to Freeform Twill

Freeform twill is an ideal point from which to embark upon our study of freeform design technique. Twill is a weave familiar to every weaver, whether beginner or advanced, and is probably the most versatile weave we encounter. Perhaps its versatility is the very reason twill adapted so well to the technique known as *damask*, which was woven in China as long ago as 3000 years, and in Europe from the 1500s. This same versatility gives rise to the contemporary translation of four-harness damask into freeform design technique, and what I call *freeform twill*.

It is necessary at this point to address a potential misunderstanding in terminology. "Damask" is a term which traditionally is reserved for a nine (or more) harness turned twill in which warp-faced and weft-faced twills are threaded to be woven simultaneously, each in a 1:4 satin weave. Of the following weaves, only the broken freeform

A small to medium size boat shuttle with pointed ends is easier to manipulate than a stick shuttle. However, the use of a stick shuttle is possible when weaving a freeform design technique. The following Photo shows the pointed shuttles used today in China with the draw loom.

Chinese draw loom shuttles.

It is also possible to design a shuttle using the lines of the Chinese shuttles. The following Photo is of a hand-crafted shuttle which I use and find ideal for the weaving of freeform design technique.

Freeform shuttle.

There are many shuttles on the market which are suitable for weaving freeform design techniques. The particular one shown in the following Photo works quite adequately, and is readily available.

Commercial shuttle.

twill, which is the four-harness version of a turned twill in satin weave, can be considered a form of damask. That, however, is as close as the following freeform twill weaves approximate the traditional technique. As you will see, the freeform twill weaves all look similar to damask as we have come to identify it. To prevent confusion, the following weaves will all be referred to as "freeform twill."

Freeform twill is a weave system which combines the weaving of a weft-faced twill and a warp-faced twill *in the same row* to form different pattern areas in the weave. *Photo 1-1* shows a contemporary piece woven in this manner.

Ph. 1-1. Freeform twill.

Traditional Twill

By way of introduction to freeform twill, the threading and treadling of the traditional warp-faced and weft-faced straight twills must be studied first. These are the two weave structures upon which most of the four-harness freeform twills are based. The threading for either of these two weaves is harnesses 1,2,3,4 repeated selvedge-to-selvedge. To weave a warp-faced twill on a rising shed loom, three harnesses must be raised at one time in each of the four rows. For a weft-faced twill, one harness is raised in each of the four rows. *Figure 1-1* details the draw-downs for the warp-faced and the weft-faced straight twills. It remains now to demonstrate the conversion of these two twill weave structures to the loom-controlled method of freeform twill.

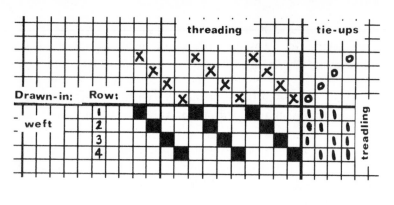

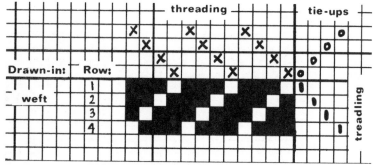

Fig. 1-1A. Twill with straight threading and warp-faced treadling (top).

Fig. 1-1B. Twill with straight threading and weft-faced treadling (bottom).

The Process of Freeform Design Technique

The procedure for weaving freeform twill will be the same for all other freeform design techniques presented. Therefore, once freeform twill is understood, there should be no problem interpreting the other techniques.

Freeform Twill With Straight Threading and Treadling

According to the definition of freeform design technique, the threading is the first consideration for conversion of warp- and weft-faced twills to freeform twill. The threading sequence must be one which is repeated selvedge-to-selvedge. Since the threading used for both the warp- and weft-faced twills in *Figure 1-1* is already the same single threading sequence repeated selvedge-to-selvedge, this threading on harnesses 1,2,3,4 will be appropriate for freeform twill.

To weave in the technique of freeform design, it is necessary to treadle for both the warp- and weft-faced weave structures in the same row. As an example, lift harness 1 for a weft-faced twill and move the shuttle partway through the shed. Then, with the shuttle still in the shed, change the treadling and lift harnesses 1,2&3 for a warp-faced twill, and continue moving the shuttle through this new shed. This is what freeform design technique is: the weaving of one weave structure by lifting one harness combination for part of a row, and changing the treadling to another harness combination, with the shuttle still in the shed, to produce another weave structure. Depending on the complexity of the design being woven, these two harness combinations may be alternated from one to the other as many times as desired while the shuttle travels from one selvedge to the other.

Manipulating the Shuttle with Freeform Design Technique

As the treadling is changed with the shuttle moving from selvedge-to-selvedge, there are a few hints which could be of help in manipulating the shuttle in this somewhat different manner. With the shuttle in the shed at the point where treadling is to be changed, move the shuttle ahead and bring the tip of the shuttle up and out of the shed.

Shuttle in position to change treadling.

Now change the treadling. Place the index finger of the hand which is not holding the shuttle down into the shed at the point where the shuttle emerged. This helps to mark the desired point of change.

Treadling change marked.

Gently pull the shuttle back and down into the new shed, entering this shed at the point where your finger is separating the warp.

Shuttle entering new shed.

If you are working with a warp that is wider than twelve inches, it will not be possible to control the shuttle by holding it in the conventional manner. Instead, it will be necessary to maneuver the shuttle by reaching down through the top layer of the warp. The following Photo shows the hand position for best control of the shuttle. This method of advancing the shuttle will not distort the warp in any way, although you may find it best to loosen the warp tension by one notch. Also, you may wish to remove any jewelry as it may catch on the warp!

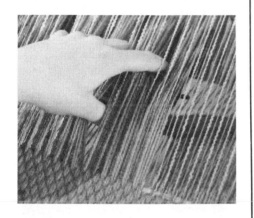

Shuttle maneuvered in a wide shed.

This entire procedure may seem a bit cumbersome at first, but as you take this technique to the loom, you will find it to be a speedy and efficient method of advancing the shuttle when weaving in freeform design technique.

The two harness combinations presented constitute one row. It takes four rows to weave four-harness freeform twill, and each of the four rows is assigned one pair of harness combinations, one for weft-faced twill and one for warp-faced twill. If these four rows with their pairs of harness combinations are treadled in order from 1 through 4, the result is straight freeform twill. The four rows of treadling (with their pairs of harness combinations) for freeform twill woven with straight treadling are detailed in *Figure 1-2A*.

Figure 1-2B shows, in a draw-down, the same four rows with pairs of harness combinations for freeform twill woven with straight treadling.

Freeform twill with straight threading and treadling sequence.

Fig. 1-2A. Table of Harness Combinations and Treadling (right).

Fig. 1-2B. Draw-down (below).

Row:		Harness Combinations:		
1		1 ← OR →		1, 2, 3
2		2 ← OR →		1, 2, 4
3		3 ← OR →		1, 3, 4
4		4 ← OR →		2, 3, 4
		weft-faced		warp-faced

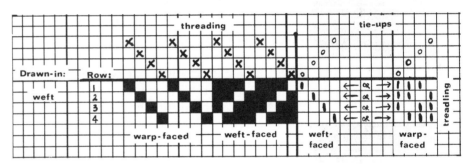

The order in which the warp- and weft-faced harness combinations are treadled results in straight twill diagonals, with the direction of one diagonal opposing the other. This line opposition is helpful in visually identifying pattern areas, and can be found in traditional draw loom damask as well as in contemporary freeform twill.

A close-up of part of *Photo 1-1* is shown in *Photo 1-2*. If this is the design motif to be used for weaving, note that the left side in the photo is woven in straight warp-faced twill, the middle section in straight weft-faced twill, and the right side again in straight warp-faced twill. The weaving begins with Row 1 and with the shuttle at the right selvedge. The first harness combination is warp-faced, lifting harnesses 1, 2&3, and the shuttle passes as far through

Ph. 1-2. Freeform twill. Enlargement of one area of Photo 1-1.

the shed as the pattern dictates. At that point where the pattern changes to weft-faced, the treadling is changed to the weft-faced harness combination of Row 1 (lifting only harness 1), and the shuttle continues, but now in the weft-faced shed. The last change is back to the warp-faced harness combination for Row 1 (lifting harnesses 1, 2&3 again), and the shuttle proceeds across the remainder of the shed.

Row 2 begins at the left selvedge with the second warp-faced harness combination (lifting harnesses 1, 2&4). When the pattern changes to weft-faced, the treadling changes to the second weft-faced harness combination (lifting harness 2). Then the treadling is changed back to the Row 2 warp-faced harness combination (lifting harnesses 1, 2&4 again) and the shuttle proceeds across the remainder of the shed.

In Row 3, the shuttle is at the right selvedge. Lift harnesses 1,3&4 to accommodate the warp-faced design, and weave to the point in the shed where the design changes to weft-faced. Lift harness 3, and move the shuttle to the next change in the design. Lift harnesses 1,3&4 again (warp-faced), and take the shuttle to the left selvedge.

In Row 4, beginning at the left selvedge, lift harnesses 2,3&4 to accommodate the warp-faced design. Move the shuttle through the shed to the point where the treadling changes. Lift harness 4 and weave in this weft-faced shed to the next place where the treadling changes. Lift harnesses 2,3&4 again, and move the shuttle to the right selvedge. This four-row process is repeated throughout the piece with treadling changes made in each row according to the pattern.

To weave an area without any pattern, just background, simply weave the appropriate treadling sequence selvedge-to-selvedge. For the design in *Photo 1-1*, this means treadling the warp-faced harness combinations in the following order: harnesses 1,2,3; 1,2,4; 1,3,4; 2,3,4.

Freeform Twill With Straight Threading and Broken Treadling

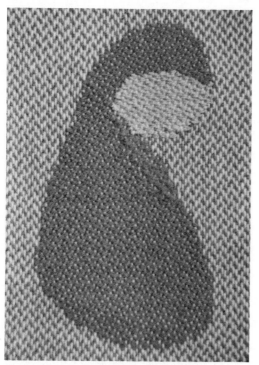

The broken twill weave structure is an important variation, and is the freeform twill which comes closest to traditional damask. The same four rows that were used for the weaving of freeform straight twill are used for freeform broken twill, and each row is assigned the same pair of harness combinations for the warp- and weft-faced weave structures. To form a broken twill instead of straight, Rows 2 & 3, with their pairs of harness com-

Ph. 1-3. Freeform twill with straight threading and broken treadling sequence.

Treadling As-Drawn-In Warp End-By-End

The term "treadling as-drawn-in" is the translation of an early American term "tromp as writ". These terms refer to the technique of assigning a harness combination to each harness or group of harnesses in the threading. The threading sequence is then followed, treadling the appropriate harness combination for each harness or group of harnesses in the threading. A typical "Key" for treadled as-drawn-in follows:

harness 1-1&2 harness combination
    "   2-2&3   "
    "   3-3&4   "
    "   4-4&1   "

In the above Key, each harness combination is assigned to a single harness, and, therefore, to a single warp end. This is referred to as the "thread-by-thread" method of treadling as-drawn-in. Referring to the above Key, the treadling for harness 1 is harness combination 1&2, the treadling for harness 2 is harness combination 2&3, and so forth. The threading repeat for a return point twill is harnesses 1,2,3,4,3,2. The treadling for those six rows, according to the Key, is therefore: harness combinations 1&2, 2&3, 3&4, 4&1, 3&4, 2&3.

When twill is treadled as-drawn-in, the thread-by-thread method is usually used. The assigned harness combinations for twill may be weft-faced, warp-faced, or a balanced weave structure. The above Key is for a balanced weave structure. If the weave structure is to be weft-faced, harness 1 is assigned harness combination 1; harness 2 = 2; harness 3 = 3; and harness 4 = 4. For a warp-faced weave structure, harness 1 is assigned harness combination 1,2&3; harness 2 = 2,3,&4; harness 3 = 3,4&1; and harness 4 = 4,1&2. Actually, any sequence of harness combinations can be assigned to the harnesses. The above sequences establish the most obvious assignments.

Figuring How Many Ends Per Inch

Charts are available for natural yarns which inform us that "10/2 cotton should be sett at 24 epi, 3/12 wool should be sett at 18 epi", and so forth. But what about synthetic yarns, mixed warps, or unknown fiber content? The following method is one which allows the weaver to determine the number of epi suitable for any yarn.

Wrap the yarn in question around a yardstick, pushing the turns as closely together as possible without having the threads overlap. Wrap one-half inch of warp in this manner. Whatever number of closely wrapped warp threads occurs in the one-half inch is the appropriate sett per inch for plain weave. "Plain weave" implies that a yarn will be used for weft which is close in size to the warp, and that approximately the same number of rows will be woven per inch as there are warp ends per inch. If you intend to weave twill, the sett should be one or two ends per inch closer than for plain weave. If you wish a loose weave, or if you plan to use a heavier weft yarn, the sett should be fewer epi than for plain weave.

Simplified Attachment of the Warp to the Front Apron Rod

Many weavers use the "weaver's knot" to secure the warp to the cloth beam apron rod (or the warp beam apron rod if beaming is done from front to back). It can be difficult to obtain even warp tension selvedge-to-selvedge using this method, and considerable retying may be necessary.

The use of a continuous cord to affix the warp to the cloth or warp beam apron rod is simple, speedy and assures an even warp tension.

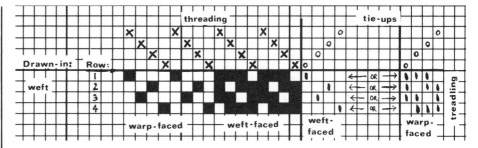

Freeform twill with straight threading and broken treadling.

Fig. 1-3A. Draw-down (above).

Fig. 1-3B. Table of Harness Combinations and Treadling (left).

Row:			Harness Combinations:
1	1	← OR →	1, 2, 3
2	3	← OR →	1, 3, 4
3	2	← OR →	1, 2, 4
4	4	← OR →	2, 3, 4
	weft-faced		warp-faced

binations, simply trade places. The draw-down of broken freeform twill is detailed in *Figure 1-3A*. The Table of Harness Combinations and Treadling for the four rows is detailed in *Figure 1-3B*. The figure of the Madonna in *Photo 1-3* is woven in freeform broken twill.

Freeform twill, woven as a broken weave structure, is particularly suited to the development of curved lines in a design. Since there is no clear diagonal line in the weave, it is visually easier to follow a curved line as well as to weave it. In many pieces, a distinct diagonal line might well detract from the design. *Photo 1-4* shows a piece in which one half is woven as a straight warp- and weft-faced weave structure, and the other half as a broken weave structure. Notice with a curved design such as the one used in both halves of *Photo 1-4*, that the half woven as a broken weave structure has cleaner design edges than the half woven with straight treadling.

Ph. 1-4. Freeform twill with straight threading. The lower half of the piece is woven with straight treadling; the upper half with broken.

Freeform Twill with Straight Threading and Combined Straight and Broken Treadling

So far, the straight and broken freeform twills have been presented as two separate entities. There is no reason, however, why the two weaves cannot be combined in one piece; a broken warp-faced twill with a straight weft-faced twill or vice versa. *Figure 1-4A&B* gives the Table of Harness Combinations and Treadling for straight and broken twill woven simultaneously in freeform twill. Notice while the rows are still numbered from 1 to 4, that the pairs of harness combinations for Rows 2 and 3 are not the same as for straight and broken freeform twill. *Photo 1-5* shows a piece in which one half of the piece is woven with a straight twill background and broken twill design area, and the other half is woven with a broken twill background area and straight twill design area. Again notice, with a curved design motif, that the half woven with the design area in broken twill results in design lines which appear much smoother than the half in which the straight twill is used in the design motif area.

Once the warp is threaded and sley-ed: 1)*Knot the warp ends into groups of not more than one sleyed inch of warp per knot. Tie the knots as evenly as possible across the warp.* 2)*Adjust the position of the knots and apron rod so that all knots are a minimum of 1" from the apron rod.* 3)*Secure a strong cord, four times the weaving width, to the apron rod at the right of the warp.* 4)*Split the first group of warp threads and pass the cord through, just above the knot.* 5)*Put the cord around the rod, pulling the cord and warp threads taut.* 6)*Repeat this process until all of the knots have been accommodated.* 7)*Tie the cord securely to the rod at the left of the warp. Tighten the warp to weaving tension.*

Row:	Harness Combinations:
1	1 ← OR → 1, 2, 3
2	3 ← OR → 1, 2, 4
3	2 ← OR → 1, 3, 4
4	4 ← OR → 2, 3, 4
	broken weft-faced — straight warp-faced

Row:	Harness Combinations:
1	1 ← OR → 1, 2, 3
2	2 ← OR → 1, 3, 4
3	3 ← OR → 1, 2, 4
4	4 ← OR → 2, 3, 4
	straight weft-faced — broken warp-faced

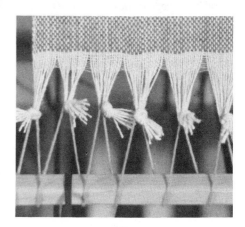

Warp tied to the front apron rod.

Freeform twill with straight threading and combined treadling.

Fig. 1-4A. Weft-faced broken treadling combined with warp-faced straight treadling (above left).

Fig. 1-4B. Warp-faced broken treadling combined with weft-faced straight treadling (above right).

Ph. 1-5. Woven sample in which the piece is woven in weft-faced straight and warp-faced broken (left).

8)*To adjust the warp tension, pull the cord tighter at those places where the warp is too loose, and distribute the cord length to the points where the warp is too tight.*

Adjusting the warp tension.

Additional Twill Treadlings with Straight Threading

In addition to broken and straight twill treadling sequences, there are several others which can be used effectively in freeform twill pieces with a straight twill threading. Each of the treadling sequences mentioned uses the same four rows and pairs of warp- and weft-faced harness combinations as designated to straight and

When weaving on a four-harness loom, it is easiest to tie the harnesses directly, that is, to tie each harness to a separate treadle. Your feet can treadle any harness combination possible for four harnesses. If there are six treadles on your four-harness loom, tie up the four middle treadles. Your feet will become accustomed to searching out the correct treadling, especially if you weave without shoes!

However, if you prefer to weave using multiple tie-ups, in which more than one harness is tied to one treadle, prepare the tie-ups in whatever order suits you. If you prefer the "walking" method in which the treadling sequence alternates for the left foot and then the right foot, arrange the tie-ups accordingly. If, on the other hand, you prefer to treadle with one foot for several treadlings, and then the other foot for several, arrange the tie-ups accordingly. The main concern is that the tie-ups be prepared for you and your loom. You need not feel that the stated arrangement is the one which must be used.

Warp Tension with Freeform Design Techniques

It is best to weave with the warp tension one notch looser than what you ordinarily use. This slightly looser tension allows the shuttle to be maneuvered through the treadling changes without putting undue stress on the warp threads.

"Every line we can draw in the sand has exression; and there is no body without its spirit or genius. All form is an effect of character; all condition, of the quality of life; all harmony, of health."
Ralph Waldo Emerson

broken freeform twills. The order in which the rows are woven is different, just as the order is changed to weave straight or broken freeform twill. The following are three familiar treadling sequences: RETURN POINT (Row# 1,2,3,4,3,2); GOOSE EYE (Row# 1,2,3,4, 1,2,3,4,1,4,3,2,1,4,3,2,1,4); HERRINGBONE (Row# 1,2,3,4,1,2,3,4, 2,1,4,3,2,1,4,3). *Photo 1-6* shows a sample of return point treadling with a straight twill threading.

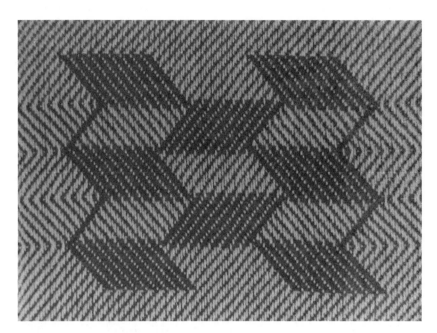

Ph. 1-6. Freeform twill with straight threading and return point treadling sequence.

Additional Twill Threadings

To carry the freeform twill concept still farther, there are many twill threadings other than the straight threading which are appropriate for freeform twill. Actually, any twill threading which can be treadled for a warp-faced and weft-faced weave structure can be used for freeform twill. The order in which the rows are woven for these different twill threadings can be any of those mentioned thus far: straight, broken, return point, goose eye, or herringbone. There are also other twill treadling sequences possible for twill, the most effective being treadled as-drawn-in.

The four pairs of warp- and weft-faced harness combinations and their designated row numbers will be the same as straight and broken freeform twills. The order in which the rows are woven is again changed. There is an almost unlimited number of possibilities for combining four-harness twill threadings and the treadling sequence of the rows.

A word of caution. Keep the weave structures simple or the weave will overpower the design and detract from, rather than enhance, the final result. The use of finer yarns and/or more subtle color shadings for warp and weft helps subdue the weave structure being woven. *Photos 1-7* and *1-8* show pieces for which the threading differs from straight, with treadling sequences and designs appropriate for the particular weave structures. A draw-down accompanies each photograph.

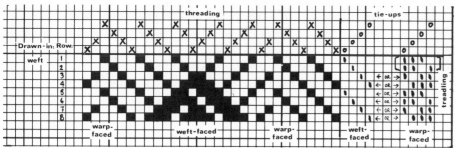

Herringbone threading and straight treadling.

Fig. 1-5. Draw-down (above).

Ph. 1-7. Woven sample. Warp runs horizontally in the photo; weft, vertically (left).

Goose Eye threading treadled as-drawn-in.

Fig. 1-6. Draw-down (below).
Ph. 1-8. Woven sample (right).

Determining the Warp Length

Avoid the frustration of having the warp end before the project — or of wondering what to do with 3 extra yards of warp! The following method should allow project and warp to finish together. Calculations are made for the warp length necessary to weave a 50" scarf as the steps are given.

1. Project length - the desired length of the project.
   Scarf - 50"
2. Hems or other necessary woven finishing.
   Scarf - 0
3. Shrinkage (if appropriate). Add #s 1 & 2 together and take 10% of the total.
   Scarf - 5"
4. Add numbers 1,2&3 together to find the weaving length.
   Scarf - 55"
5. Warp take-up (the amount of warp undulation in the weaving as the weft is accommodated). Add 10% of #4, rounded to next higher number.
   Scarf - 6"
6. Sample for records - 10-15"
   Scarf - 10"
7. Loom waste (knots and heading at the beginning of the warp, and the end of the warp which cannot be woven). Table loom, add 16"; small floor loom, add 20"; large

floor loom, add 25-30".
   Scarf - 20"
The warp length — the sum of #s 4,5,6&7.
   Scarf - 91" warp (2.5 yards)
   The total number of yards necessary to wind the warp is found by multiplying the number of warp ends times the warp length. If the scarf in question is 12" wide in the reed with, say, 20 ends per inch, the total number of warp ends for the project is 240. The total number of yards needed to wind the warp is: 240 x 2.5 = 600 yards.

If the weft yarn is approximately the same size as the warp, and the sett is to square, the amount of weft yarn needed is 2/3 that of warp (400 yards for the scarf).

"You had better learn to accept all the small misfits and the trivial annoyances of life as a matter of course. To allow them to receive attention beyond their deserts is to wear the web of your life to the warp. Be on the lookout for the great joys, and never let mosquitoes worry you into a passion."
           Elbert Hubbard

Twill weave structures are particularly enhanced in freeform design technique when either the warp- or weft-faced area involves a broken treadling sequence. In *Figure 1-7*, a weft-faced broken treadling sequence is combined with warp-faced treadling as-drawn-in for goose eye threading. Notice that, with the combining of two different weave structures, it is necessary to change the pairing of harness combinations, and more than four rows are necessary to complete the treadling sequence. A sample in which these two treadling sequences are combined is shown in *Photo 1-9*.

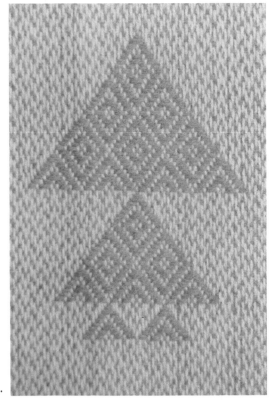

Goose Eye threading with combined treadling as-drawn-in and broken.

Fig. 1-7. Draw-down (below).

Ph. 1-9. Woven sample (right).

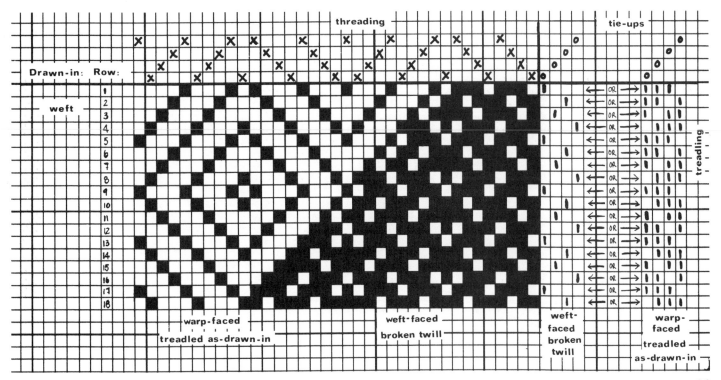

Eighteen rows are shown in *Figure 1-7*. This number of rows completes the treadling as-drawn-in, but leaves the broken treadling sequence on the second treadling. Continue the broken treadling sequence as the treadling as-drawn-in begins again. At the end of the second time through the treadling as-drawn-in, both treadling sequences will be completed.

Suitable Projects

Freeform twill is a light weight, drapable material with uses ranging as broadly as those of traditional twill. Yardage, upholstery, accessories, wallhangings and table linens are but a few of the possibilities. Yarns used for freeform twill should be those most appropriate for the article being woven and may be light to heavy weight. In general, the warp and weft yarns should be of the same weight as one another, and should be of a smooth texture in order to emphasize the weave structures. Refer to Appendix A for details.

Weave An Extra Placemat

When giving a set of placemats as a gift, or when weaving a set for your own use, weave 5 placemats instead of 4, 9 instead of 8. That extra mat is nice for the center of the table. And should one mat be lost to a stain that will not release or a tear, the set has not been lost!

"I met an aged man, and asked him for the time. 'Time', he replied, 'is the warp of life. Tell the young to weave it well.'"

anonymous

(Above)
Ph. 1-10. Wallhanging woven in 40/3 cotton with straight threading and treadling. Woven by Mimi Pope.

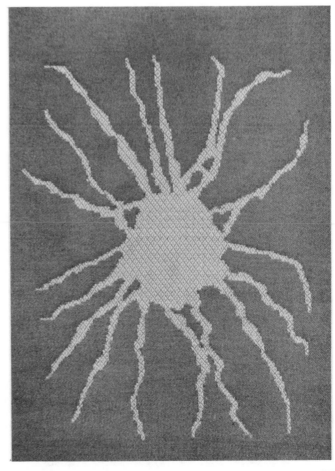

(Above)
Ph. 1-11. Pillow of medium weight wool and 5/2 Verel with straight threading and treadling. Weft inlay is used for the sheep. Woven by Lois Crocker.

(Right)
Ph. 1-12. Sampler in 9-harness freeform twill. This piece is included as an example of contemporary damask. It is woven in 80/2 cotton with return point threading, and treadling as-drawn-in combined with broken. Woven by Jim Ahrens.

(Right)
Ph. 1-13. Scarf of medium weight wool with return point threading and treadling. Woven by Ann Christensen.

(Above)
Ph. 1-14. Enlargement of one area of the wool scarf.

(Below)
Ph. 1-15. Sampler woven in 5/2 Verel (cotton count) with straight threading and combined straight and broken treadling. Woven by Mugs O'Toole.

(Left)
Ph. 1-16. Sampler woven in 5/2 Verel with return point twill in both threading and treadling. Woven by Ann Christensen.

(Left)
Ph. 1-17. Bookmark woven in 80/2 cotton with straight threading and treadling. Woven by Jo Ann Nelson.

(Right)
Ph. 1-18. Wallhanging entitled "Mountains" with undulating twill threading and straight treadling. Woven in 40/3 cotton - by the author.

(Lower right)
Ph. 1-19. Enlargement of an area of the wallhanging entitled "Mountains".

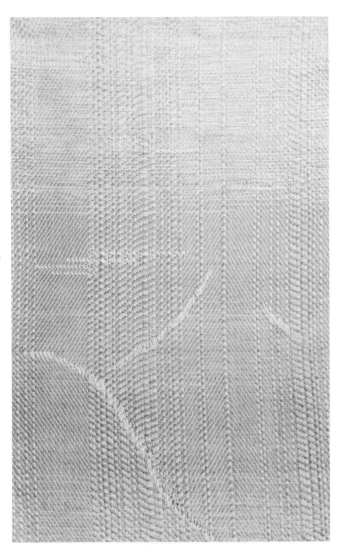

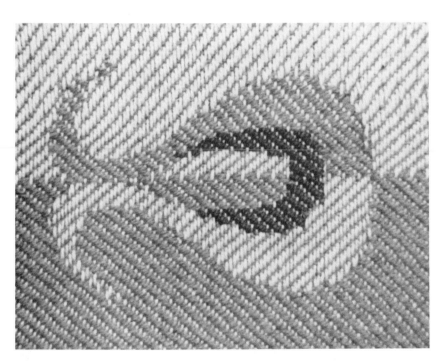

Ph. 1-20. Sampler woven in 5/2 Verel using straight threading and treadling. Weft inlay yarns are included. Woven by Sue Koski.

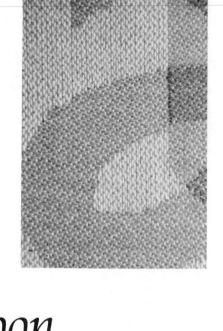

2.

Tools of the Trade
Weft Inlay & The Cartoon

Now that you have experienced freeform twill and have an understanding of the way in which freeform design technique is woven, there are two skills which are helpful to know. The first is the technique of laying in additional weft yarns, and the second is the use of the cartoon. As you study additional freeform techniques, the knowledge of weft inlay and cartooning will afford you creative lattitude.

The Addition of Weft Inlay Yarns

Ph. 2-1. Freeform twill with no inlay yarns.

It is possible to enhance a design as it is woven by a method called "weft inlay", in which different colored and/or textured yarns are added to the selvedge-to-selvedge pattern weft yarn. The method for adding weft inlay yarns is the same for all of the freeform design techniques presented in this book. Therefore, it will be a simple matter to apply the method described for freeform twill to other freeform design techniques. *Photo 2-1* shows a piece woven first without weft inlay, and *Photo 2-2* is your design on a piece of paper, four or five times. Color each of these drawings using different combinations and · arrangements of color within the piece. By comparing the drawings, it should not be difficult to select the preferred colors and arrangement.

If the design is too intricate to draw or trace, make one copy on a copier. Place tracing paper over the design and color on the tracing paper. The use of several pieces of tracing paper will give you several combinations of color for comparison.

Use Only Three Colors

The use of more than three colors from the color wheel in one piece can result in a visual "muddying" of the colors into a brown. One color should be used for approximately two-thirds of the piece. Use a second color in approximately one-third of the piece. A third color can be used as an accent, and is often the complement of either the main or secondary color. Shades and tints of the colors may be used, as may black, grey and white.

The combining of colors in this manner occurs in weaving in two ways. Colors may be combined in the warp, with one of the colors also used as weft; or in the weft with one of the colors as warp. If the colors are to be combined in the warp, one color is selected as the main one and should account for approximately two-thirds of the warp. The second color accounts for roughly one-third of the warp, and the accent appears only occasionally. The main color may include several different yarns which are shades or tints of the chosen color. This is also true with the second color. The accent usually involves only one yarn.

As an example, red may be selected as the main color and may include maroons to pinks. If blue is the second color, navy to light blue

Ph. 2-2. Freeform twill with weft inlay yarns added.

of the same piece woven with weft inlay.

The yarn to be used for weft inlay should be the same size or slightly finer than the selvedge-to-selvedge pattern weft. Start with approximately one yard of yarn for each area of weft inlay. New yarns may be added as needed. No shuttle is necessary.

Before adding weft inlay yarns, the selvedge-to-selvedge pattern weft is woven, treadling the warp-faced harness combination in any area where the weft inlay yarn is to be added. For example, if you are adding weft inlay to Row 1 of straight freeform twill, the selvedge-to-selvedge weft yarn is woven first, lifting harness 1 for areas to be woven weft-faced, and harnesses 1,2&3 for areas to be woven warp-faced. Lift harnesses 1,2&3 in areas where weft inlay yarns are to be added.

When the selvedge-to-selvedge pattern weft has been woven through the shed, treadle the appropriate weft-faced harness combination for the row just woven. For Row 1 of straight freeform twill, lift harness 1. Place the weft inlay yarn under the weaving and bring it up into the shed where it is to be laid in, through the shed however far it is to go, and down to the underside again. The inlay yarn is worked totally from the underside of the piece. If there is more than one weft inlay yarn to be added, continue, with harness 1 lifted, to place each weft inlay yarn into place in the shed, working each time from the underside of the piece. *Photo 2-3* shows the passage of the weft inlay yarn and the position of the hands in placing the yarn.

Each row is woven in this manner, with the selvedge-to-selvedge pattern weft woven first, and the weft inlay yarns then worked from the underside of the piece. The weft-faced harness combination lifted for the weft inlay will always be the same as the weft-faced harness combination of the selvedge-to-selvedge pattern just woven. Remember, the selvedge-to-selvedge pattern weft is treadled using the warp-faced harness combination in all areas where weft inlay yarns are to be added.

Ph. 2-3. The placement of a weft inlay yarn.

When using the same weft inlay color in more than one area, it is best to use a separate length of yarn for each one. If a single yarn is carried on the back of the weaving from one area to another, it may cause puckering and distortion of the finished piece. Because the weft inlay yarns advance from one row to the next on the back of the weaving, the piece will no longer be totally reversible.

The Cartoon

Developing a Cartoon

With freeform design techniques, it may be somewhat threatening to be given a threading, two harness combinations and the instructions to "weave a design". Probably the most helpful tool for confronting this situation is the use of the cartoon. A small design is made before the weaving is started. It is enlarged, and is placed under the warp to be used as a guide throughout the weaving. This eliminates guesswork about the final result, and may offer considerable security for first attempts at freeform design technique.

The more familiar you are with the weave for which you are designing, the more quickly design ideas will develop. It is helpful to design the cartoon after weaving a sampler in which possible color and yarn combinations are tried.

Start with a small sketch. That in itself may be threatening! However, only certain designs will seem appropriate if you keep the weave structure and the woven article in mind. A few sources for design ideas are: books of borders, calendar pictures, needlepoint pattern books, wallpaper samples, or pictures which have been cut out and saved, all of which should be kept together in folders or scrapbook. (Resolve to start an *idea book* if you do not already have one!)

Once an idea for a design has been found, the next step is to allow the idea to grow. Draw 20 or so boxes on a piece of graph paper, close to the scale of the piece you plan to weave. Make the boxes about 2" wide and however long they must be to have them drawn to scale. For example, in planning a blanket 36"x40" to be woven in freeform design technique, the idea boxes will be almost square, 2" x 2 1/8".

yarns can be considered. Occasionally, an olive green yarn is introduced as the accent. Green is the complement of red and its use will make the red appear brighter, more intense. Off-whites and deep charcoal grey might be added to visually separate color areas.

The second way in which yarns are combined in weaving is according to area. Tapestries, double weave, and weft inlay are techniques which isolate colors into specific areas of a piece. Again, no more than three colors should be used. One area and color should account for roughly two-thirds of a piece, a second for one-third of the piece. The accent appears occasionally in any of the areas.

Color Terms

Color Wheel - *a specific arrangement of the twelve colors which form the natural spectrum. This arrangement includes the primary, secondary and tertiary colors.*

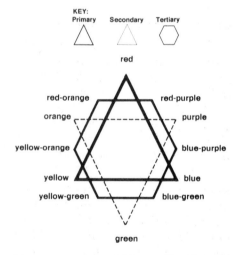

Hue - *a color with specific characteristics and a designated name (red, green, blue, etc.).*
Primary color - *red, yellow, blue. The three colors to which no other color has been added in their formation, and from which all other colors are made.*
Secondary color - *orange, green, violet. A color formed by combining two primary colors.*

Tertiary color - *yellow-green, green-blue, blue-violet, violet-red, red-orange, orange-yellow. A color formed by combining a primary and adjacent secondary color.*

Monochromatic - *two or more shades of one color.*

Analogous - *two colors next to one another on the color wheel.*

Complements - *red & green, yellow & violet, blue & orange. Two colors opposite one another on the color wheel.*

Value - *the lightness or darkness of a color, according to a scale, ranging from white to black.*

Tint - *a color made lighter by adding white.*

Shade - *a color made darker by adding black.*

Intensity - *a color made darker by the addition of its complement. The resulting color appears brighter than if black is added.*

Consider the Cartoon Width

The selvedges of most weaving pull in. Keep this fact in mind when planning a piece for which a cartoon will be used. Make the cartoon the width of the piece, not the warp. Twill weaves pull in a little more than 1" per foot; plain weaves 1" per foot. Weft yarns with stretch will alter the width of a piece considerably, and shrinkage must be taken into consideration. The only weave techniques which do not lose any width are those involving few ends per inch and a firmly packed weft, or the use of a weft yarn with no give.

"Habit is a cable; we weave a thread of it every day, and at last we cannot break it." Horace Mann

Sketch a design in one box. Do not erase, but progress to the next box with a new or revised design. The idea will develop and change as more boxes are used, until a satisfactory design emerges. *Figure 2-1* shows an idea sheet for a small blanket.

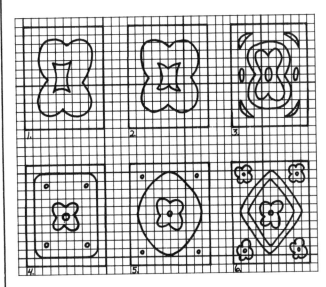

Fig. 2-1. Idea sheet for a small blanket.

Once a design is created, enlarge it to at least twice the size of the small sketch. This is the drawing from which the design is transferred to the full-size cartoon. Fold the drawing into quarters both

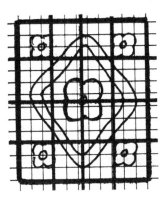

Fig. 2-2. Drawing for a cartoon divided into sixteenths.

vertically and horizontally *(Figure 2-2)*.

Cut a piece of paper the size your cartoon is to be. Shelf paper works well for a cartoon, as does brown wrapping paper. Probably the best is the commercial nonwoven fabric used for tracing patterns. Fold this paper into quarters both vertically and horizontally, just as you did the small design. Starting with a corner square, transfer the design appearing in that square on the small design to the corresponding square of the large cartoon. Move from one square to the next, transferring the entire design to the cartoon. If the design is complex or the squares are too large to allow the detail of the design to be transferred easily, fold each section of the small design and cartoon in half horizontally and vertically.

Outline the design with a heavy black line and fill in the design with colored pencils to identify design areas. Draw a dark line down the center of the cartoon, and draw in several horizontal lines which go from one edge of the cartoon to the other. The vertical line helps keep the cartoon centered, while the horizontal lines keep the cartoon straight with the weaving edge. The cartoon is now finished *(Figure 2-3)*.

Fig. 2-3. Finished cartoon.

Before attaching the cartoon to the weaving, it is important to roll it tightly with the design side out. This allows the cartoon to bend when the beater is used. Place the cartoon in position under the weaving using the vertical and horizontal lines to align it correctly. Pin the cartoon in place about 2" from the weaving edge, using three or four long "t" or corsage pins. Roll the excess length of long cartoons and secure with paper clips at either edge.

Weaving With a Cartoon

With the cartoon in place, begin weaving, following the design changes as they occur. In a row which involves treadling changes, move the shuttle through the shed just beyond the point where the treadling is to change. Bring the tip of the shuttle forward and out of the shed as described on page 26 of *INSIGHTS* in Chapter One. Place the hand not holding the shuttle under the cartoon, pressing the cartoon up against the warp. This indicates exactly where the treadling should change. *Photo 2-4* shows a cartoon pinned in place, with one hand positioning it against the warp.

Ph. 2-4. Cartoon pinned and held in place.

Keeping an eye on the place at which the treadling changes, release the cartoon, and, with the same hand which held the cartoon, place your finger down through the top shed to mark the place where the treadling changes. Change the treadling. Pull the shuttle back and down into the new shed, and proceed through the shed to the next treadling change. Repeat the process.

When advancing the warp, the beginning of the cartoon must fall between the front beam and the harnesses. It is almost impossible to keep the cartoon aligned properly once it has traveled with

Using a Second Cartoon

If a design contains intricate lines which are difficult to follow when using a cartoon under the warp, it may be desirable to add a second cartoon on top of the warp. This second cartoon is drawn only for the area of the design which is complex, and is a mirror image of the main cartoon. The second cartoon is pinned to the top surface of the weaving with the outlined design against the weaving. When a harness combination is treadled, fold the second cartoon back just to the edge of the weaving. The exact place where the treadling should be changed will be clearly visible at the fold of the cartoon.

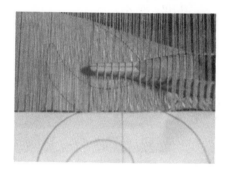

Second cartoon in position.

"If a man does not keep pace with his companions, perhaps it is because he hears a different drummer. Let him step to the music which he hears, however measured or far away. It is not important that he should mature as soon as an apple tree, or an oak. Shall he turn his spring into summer? If the condition of things which we were made for is not yet — what is any reality which we can substitute?"
Henry David Thoreau

The Cartoon Relative to Yarn Size

When planning a cartoon, it is important to be aware of the relationship between the size of the yarns and the design. More intricate design lines may require the use of finer yarns. If large yarns are preferred, consider enlarging the cartoon and the piece, if necessary, to accommodate these yarns. If yarns are too large for the design being woven, a smooth design edge will be difficult to obtain, especially if curved lines are involved.

"Originality is simply a fresh pair of eyes."   T. W. Higginson

the weaving over the front beam. Roll and secure any excess length of cartoon with paper clips to keep it out of your way.

If a wide cartoon is used, it may be awkward to bring the cartoon into position for each row, just as it is difficult to manipulate the shuttle with a wide piece. You will recall from *INSIGHTS* of Chapter 1 that, when weaving a wide freeform piece, the shuttle is maneuvered by reaching down through the top layer of warp. The same is true with a wide cartoon. It is necessary to reach down through the entire warp and pull the desired part of the cartoon into position, creasing the cartoon in the process. A wide cartoon may be folded and creased at 1" intervals before being attached to the weaving to facilitate its manipulation. *Photo 2-5* shows this method of bringing a wide cartoon up against the weaving as the

Ph. 2-5. Positioning a wide cartoon.

shuttle is moved through the row. Advancing the shuttle and positioning the cartoon by reaching down through the warp will not distort the warp, and makes the maneuvering of both shuttle and a wide cartoon a simple matter. However, it does take some time to adapt oneself to this somewhat unorthodox approach. Loosen the warp tension one notch more than is usual for freeform design technique, and be sure to remove jewelry before working with the shuttle and cartoon in this manner!

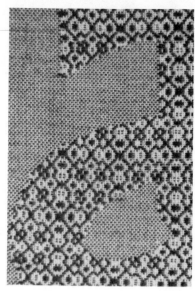

3.

Freeform Overshot

Traditional Overshot

Many weavers become acquainted with overshot early in their weaving experience. The pattern created by the threading and treadling of this weave can be very beautiful indeed. The symmetry and balance of a single pattern repeat is the essence of the true beauty of overshot. Study just one pattern repeat or, better still, try weaving just one or several repeats by the weft inlay method. The frustration is well worth the outcome. But frustrating it is!

Freeform design technique allows individual pattern repeats to be woven wherever desired—without the frustration! *Figure 3-1* details a draw-down of traditional honeysuckle overshot threading. *Photo 3-1* shows a piece threaded for honeysuckle and woven traditionally in an overall pattern design.

Fig. 3-1. Traditional honeysuckle overshot.

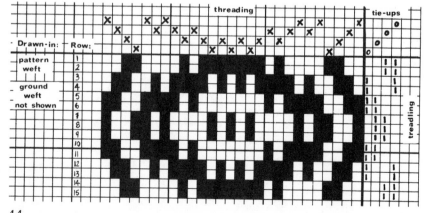

Miniature Environment for Testing Ideas

It is often difficult to tell how a wallhanging or rug will look in the environment for which it is woven until after it is off the loom and actually placed. It may then be too late to correct misjudgements!

The use of a miniature environment can solve many problems before they are woven into the piece. Make a three-sided room out of plywood or heavy cardboard, scaled 1" per foot. Add the same scale dollhouse furniture to the room roughly duplicating the environment into which the woven piece will be used.

Then weave a piece, also in a scale of 1" per foot. Not only must the design be to scale, but also the yarns which are used. While the yarns may not be exactly to scale, they should be fine enough to create the desired size effect.

Once the piece is woven, photograph it in the environment. These photographs allow the viewer to observe the environment as an isolated set without the interference of full-scale surroundings. A miniature environment including a woven wallhanging is shown. The small hanging measures 3 1/2" by 5". The piece was actually woven 40" by 60".

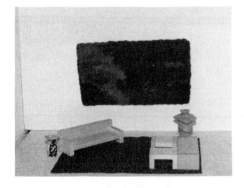

A miniature environment including a wallhanging which has been woven to scale to determine the effect of design and colors before weaving the full-size piece.

Ph. 3-1. Traditional honey-suckle overshot.

Ph. 3-2. Isolated honeysuckle pattern woven in freeform design technique.

In traditional overshot, isolated overshot motifs are created by the weft inlay method, and the pattern weft yarn travels only through those areas applicable for pattern development. This can result in weft build-up and distortion of the piece. This potential hazard is totally eliminated by the freeform method of weaving isolated pattern motifs. There is no weft build-up because the pattern shuttle travels selvedge-to-selvedge, even when only a few pattern motifs are being developed. The traditional honeysuckle threading, woven in freeform overshot with only a few of the overshot pattern repeats developed, is shown in *Photo 3-2*.

Freeform Overshot

Just as with freeform twill, the first consideration for converting overshot to a freeform design technique is the threading. The unit of threading to be repeated selvedge-to-selvedge for freeform overshot is the traditional threading sequence for whichever overshot weave has been selected. For honeysuckle, the threading unit is the traditional 26 thread sequence.

As with traditional overshot, there are two weft yarns used in freeform overshot: a *pattern weft* which is twice the size of the warp and of a contrasting color, and a *ground weft* (tabby) which is the color and size of the warp. Since both the pattern and ground wefts in freeform overshot involve the use of a plain weave structure, differentiation will be made by referring to the weave structure as "plain weave" when used with the pattern weft, and "ground" when used as the weft which is thrown selvedge-to-selvedge between pattern rows.

The next consideration for conversion to freeform is the harness combinations to be used with each of the weft yarns. The pattern weft, which forms the overshot, is the weft with which we are concerned for developing freeform design. The two weave structures considered with respect to the pattern weft in freeform overshot are plain weave (harness combinations 1&3, 2&4), and overshot (harness combinations 1&2, 2&3, 3&4, 4&1). Both weave structures produce balanced weaves—an equal amount of warp and weft shows on both sides of the fabric. However, as the weave structures differ distinctly, two design areas can be woven simultaneously, one in plain weave and one in overshot. *Figure 3-2A* details a draw-down of freeform overshot threaded for honeysuckle. The Table Of Harness Combinations And Treadling for freeform overshot is given in *Figure 3-2B.*

Consistent pairing of one overshot and one plain weave harness combination for each pattern weft row is not possible with freeform overshot. Treadling for plain weave alternates row by row between harnesses 1&3 and 2&4, while the choice of harness combinations for overshot depends on whichever traditional treadling sequence is being followed. Therefore, either of the plain weave harness combinations may be paired in a row with any one of the overshot, depending on the sequence of both overshot and plain weave treadlings.

The Visual Effect of Pattern

Horizontal lines formed by the weave structure of traditional block weaves and freeform design techniques contribute linear strength to a piece. These lines can play an important role in the design formation of such weaves as twill, Ms & Os, and Summer & Winter. If the lines produced by the weave structure are stronger than hoped for, or not strong enough, the effect of the design may be lost. The weaver must decide how strong the visual effect of the weave structure is to be.

If the visual effect is to be very much in evidence, the yarns for warp and pattern weft should contrast in value and hue. When the selected yarns for warp and pattern weft are twisted together, they should not blend, but form a "barber pole". If the visual effect of the weave structure is to be less evident in the weave, the warp and weft yarns should be closer in value to one another. A textured weft yarn will also help make the weave structure less evident.

Adapting a Design to a Specific Technique

Design choices for freeform design technique can be found in pattern books for needlepoint, crochet, and cross stitch. These designs are usually delicate, but can be modified for many of the freeform techniques.

Fig. 3-2A. Freeform overshot.

The design for the tablerunner shown in the accompanying photograph is from a book of crochet patterns. The design is delicate and requires a technique and yarns which can accommodate the lines. Freeform bronson lace woven in 5/2 Verel (cotton count) works very well.

Row:	Harness Combinations:							
1			1, 2	←	or	→	13 (24)	
2			2, 3	←	or	→	24 (13)	
3			3, 4	←	or	→	13 (24)	
4			4, 1	←	or	→	24 (13)	
			over-shot				plain weave	

Fig. 3-2B. Table of Harness Combinations and Treadling.

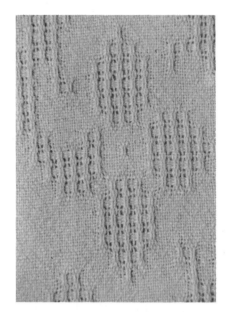

An intricate design from a book of crochet patterns adapted successfully for freeform bronson lace.

A design involving less detail is necessary to accommodate the heavy textured yarns of a technique such as broad weft Ms & Os.

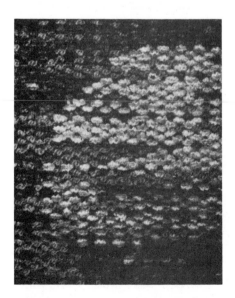

A design involving little detail used successfully in the heavier broad weft Ms & Os technique.

As with traditional overshot, the ground shuttle is thrown following *every* pattern weft row. In freeform overshot, the same harness combination is treadled for the ground row as was treadled for plain weave in the preceding pattern weft row. Treadling does not change in the ground row.

To clarify the weaving of freeform overshot, the first two rows of the draw-down shown in *Figure 3-2A* are reviewed. In Row 1 of *Figure 3-2A*, the choices for the pattern weft are harnesses 3&4 for overshot and 1&3 for plain weave. If the shuttle begins at the left selvedge, then, according to the design motif in the draw-down, plain weave harness combination 1&3 is treadled first and the shuttle moves partway through the shed to the point at which the overshot design motif is to begin. At that point, change the treadling to lift harnesses 3&4 for overshot, and take the shuttle to the right selvedge, as the design motif in the draw-down dictates. The ground weft is now woven selvedge-to-selvedge lifting harnesses 1&3, the same harness combination treadled for plain weave in Row 1. (Ground rows are not shown in the draw-down).

In Row 2, choices for the pattern weft harness combinations are 3&4 for overshot, and 2&4 for plain weave. The pattern shuttle is now at the right selvedge which means that, according to the draw-down, the first treadling is overshot harness combination 3&4. The shuttle moves to the point in the shed where the treadling changes. Lift harnesses 2&4 and take the shuttle to the left selvedge. The ground shuttle is thrown selvedge-to-selvedge lifting harnesses 2&4, the same harness combination treadled for plain weave in Row 2.

Rows 3 through 15 of *Figure 3-2A* are woven in the same manner as Rows 1 and 2, alternating, in each row, between the harness combinations for plain weave and overshot. Remember to weave a row of ground weft following every pattern row.

In areas of the fabric which require the pattern weft yarn to be woven selvedge-to-selvedge in overshot or plain weave, the treadling is selvedge-to-selvedge using the appropriate sequence of harness combinations. Ground weft is thrown as usual, after every pattern weft row.

Weft Inlay

Weft inlay yarns are added in the pattern rows of freeform overshot according to the method described in Chapter 2. Weave first with the selvedge-to-selvedge pattern weft yarn, treadling for plain weave in the areas where the weft inlay yarns are to be added. Once the pattern shuttle has reached the far selvedge, treadle the appropriate overshot harness combination for that row, and lay in the additional weft yarns from the underside of the piece. *Photo 3-3* shows a sample woven in freeform overshot with additional weft inlay yarns.

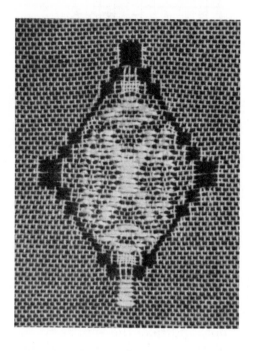

Ph. 3-3. Overshot design motif with weft inlay.

Suitable Projects

Freeform overshot is a light to medium weight weave, with good drape, which is suitable for the same range of projects as traditional overshot. Decorative bands and isolated motifs are attractive for light to medium weight clothing and accessories. The technique is also well-suited for placemats and tablerunners, pillows, bedspreads, and draperies or curtains. Refer to Appendix A for details.

The design involving fewer details would not be as interesting for a small piece woven in freeform bronson lace, as the limited number of design lines would not provide much visual interest. Likewise, if the design used for the freeform bronson lace piece were to be used with broad weft Ms & Os, the delicacy of the design would be lost completely and the detail difficult to see.

"What lies behind us and what lies before us are tiny matters compared to what lies within us."
Ralph Waldo Emerson

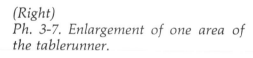

(Above)
Ph. 3-4. Placemats of 5/2 cotton threaded with an overshot block design. Woven by Doris Cox.

(Left)
Ph. 3-5. Enlargement of an area of one placemat.

(Lower right)
Ph. 3-6. Tablerunner of 5/2 Verel with "bachelor's button" threading. Woven by the author.

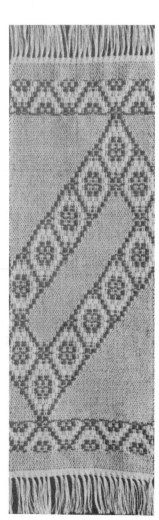

(Right)
Ph. 3-7. Enlargement of one area of the tablerunner.

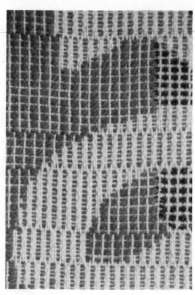

4.

Freeform Summer & Winter

Traditional Summer & Winter

Summer & Winter is another traditional 4-harness block weave which converts very nicely to freeform design technique.

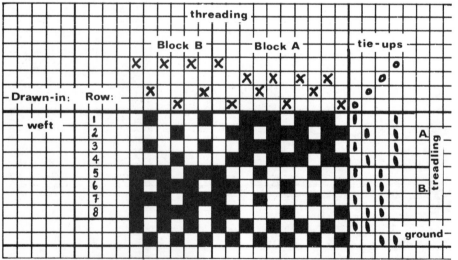

Fig. 4-1. Traditional Summer & Winter.

Ph. 4-1. Traditional Summer & Winter.

INSIGHTS

Heritage of 'Summer & Winter'

It is quite possible that the "Summer & Winter" weave as we know it was developed in this country. While similar weave structures do exist in European textiles, there is no evidence of this specific weave structure in textile archives.

If block weaves are examined, it will be noticed that most involve balanced weave structures. With single shuttle weaves, such as Ms & Os, bronson, and huck, the pattern areas appear in exactly the same position on both sides of the fabric and the weave structures are balanced. With two-shuttle block weaves such as overshot, crackle and monk's belt, the pattern appears in opposite positions on the two sides of the fabric and the weave structures are balanced.

Summer & Winter, however, is developed differently. The pattern of Summer & Winter involves a weft-faced and a warp-faced weave structure. When the pattern area is weft-faced on the fabric

50

surface, that same area is warp-faced on the back of the fabric, and vice versa. Therefore, if one block (Block "A") appears more frequently in the threading and the harness combinations for Block "A" are treadled more frequently than those of Block "B", the result is a fabric which is, essentially, weft-faced on the fabric surface and warp-faced on the underside of the fabric.

If the warp is a light color and the pattern weft is dark, the fabric will appear dark on the top surface, and light on the underside. It is surmised that the name "Summer & Winter" is in reference to coverlets which were woven to be used with the light side up in the summer, and the dark side up in the winter. Since comparatively few Summer & Winter coverlets are found today, it is assumed that they were quite special and were used only occasionally.

Pattern Rows Which Do Not Meet

A problem may arise when weaving overshot, Summer & Winter, crackle, or any other technique which involves the use of both pattern and ground weft yarns. The pattern weft rows should cover the ground in the weft-faced area, thus making the weft-faced area appear solid. When these pattern rows do not meet, the result is a visual distortion of the pattern.

Sampler in which pattern rows do not meet. The pattern looks sparse.

The two pattern weave structures to be used in converting Summer and Winter to freeform design technique are shown in *Figure 4-1*. One weave structure is weft-faced, and the second is warp-faced. In the weft-faced areas of Row 1, the pattern weft passes over three warp ends and under one. In the warp-faced areas of Row 1, the pattern weft passes under three warp ends and over one.

In Row 2, the pattern weft again passes over three warp ends and under one in the weft-faced areas, and under three warp ends and over one in the warp-faced areas. Notice within the warp-faced and the weft-faced areas that the position of the two weave structures in Row 2 directly opposes their positions in Row 1. These are the only two rows involved in weaving the pattern of traditional Summer & Winter. A ground (tabby) row is woven following every pattern row, alternating harness combinations 1&2 and 3&4. (The ground weft is not detailed in *Figure 4-1*.)

Freeform Summer & Winter

By definition, the first consideration for conversion of traditional Summer and Winter to freeform design technique is the threading. One unit of threading is selected and repeated selvedge-to-selvedge. This threading unit must contain harness combinations which can be treadled for both the warp- and weft-faced weave structures of the traditional pattern as well as the ground. If the "A" threading unit of traditional Summer & Winter, harnesses 1,3,2,3, is repeated selvedge-to-selvedge, it is possible to devise harness combinations which will produce either the warp- or weft-faced weave structure of Summer & Winter as well as plain weave. *Figure 4-2* details a draw-down of the two pattern weave structures of freeform Summer & Winter with a threading unit of harnesses 1,3,2,3.

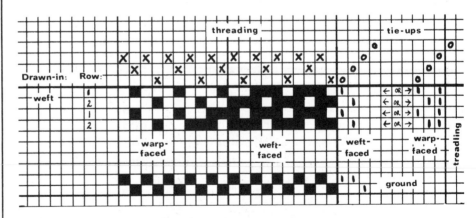

Fig. 4-2. Freeform Summer & Winter threaded 1,3,2,3.

Although this threading will work very well for freeform Summer & Winter, notice that one half the total number of warp ends is threaded on harness 3. While this is acceptable, it is better to distribute the warp ends evenly between all four harnesses whenever possible. The time required to shift extra heddles to harness 3 before threading is eliminated, and treadling is generally easier.

For these reasons, it is advantageous to seek another threading which will produce the weave structures involved in Summer &

Winter. An alternate threading unit which will weave the two pattern weave structures and the plain weave, harnesses 1,2,3,4, is shown in *Figures 4-3A&B*.

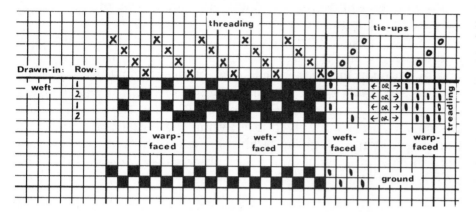

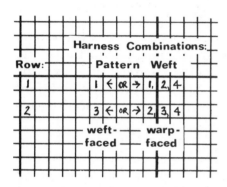

Fig. 4-3 A. Freeform Summer & Winter threaded 1,2,3,4 and treadled with a simple repeat. (above).

Fig. 4-3 B. Table of Harness Combinations and treadling (left).

The warp-faced, weft-faced and plain weave structures of *Figure 4-3A* are identical to the weave structures shown in *Figure 4-2*, which means that the alternate threading unit is successful. The ground weft is woven selvedge-to-selvedge following every pattern row, alternately lifting harness combinations 1&3 and 2&4. Remember: ground shuttle on the left, lift harnesses 2&4; ground shuttle on the right, lift harnesses 1&3. (Refer to *INSIGHTS* on page 64 for an explanation of the order of rows for the ground weft.)

Just as with traditional Summer & Winter, two weft shuttles are used to weave freeform Summer & Winter. The pattern weft yarn should be twice the size of the warp and in a contrasting color; the ground weft should be the same color and size as the warp.

The treadling for each row of pattern weft alternates between the appropriate pair of warp- and weft-faced harness combinations given in *Figure 4-3*. In pattern Row 1, lift harness 1 for a weft-faced area. When the pattern becomes warp-faced, change the treadling and lift harnesses 1,2&4. In Row 1, the treadling is alternated between these two harness combinations as many times as necessary for the design being woven. A selvedge-to-selvedge ground row follows, lifting the appropriate harness combination in the ground row sequence.

In pattern Row 2, for areas woven weft-faced, lift harness 3. For the areas to be woven warp-faced, the treadling is changed to lift harnesses 2,3&4. The treadling for Row 2 alternates between these two harness combinations to accommodate the design. Following Row 2, weave a row of ground weft selvedge-to-selvedge, treadling the alternate ground harness combination.

There are several possible solutions if the pattern rows are to meet. Try a heavier pattern weft yarn. If this does not work, try a finer ground weft yarn, first with the original pattern weft yarn, and then with the heavier one. If these attempts are not successful, it will be necessary to resley the warp for fewer ends per inch. Then, repeat the above experimentation using different combinations of pattern and ground yarn sizes.

Sampler in which the pattern rows meet. The pattern looks solid.

The Width of Samples

The rows in a narrow piece tend to compact more than the same technique woven with a wide warp. This knowledge is particularly useful when weaving a narrow sampler prior to beaming a wide warp for the same technique and yarns. If a 6" wide sampler results in the desired number of rows per inch, it may be necessary to sley the wider warp one or two fewer ends per inch to achieve the same number of rows per inch.

"Art is more godlike than science. Science discovers—Art creates."
John Opie

Simplifying a Design

It often is possible to find a suitable design for a weaving which is close to what is desired, but is too intricate or has too many colors to adapt well. A design can be simplified by using the duplicating machine. Copy the design, and then duplicate the copy. When a two-tone piece is copied, detail is removed. More detail will be removed each time a copy is duplicated. One or two duplications may be all that are necessary to reduce the design to the simplistic lines desired.

Duplicating Weavings on a Copy Machine

Are you aware that you can reproduce the weave structure of fabric on paper using a copy machine? The clearest results are of weavings with sharply contrasting colors in warp and weft. Reproducing fabrics in this way is helpful for documentation, as well as the recording of ideas for future use.

If you plan to weave a piece which is to be photographed in black and white, avoid unnecessary frustration and duplicate the yarns on the copy machine before weaving the piece. If the yarns do not develop in sharp enough contrast, you will know before the piece is woven and be able to choose other yarns.

"Choose this day the habits you would have rule over you."
Elbert Hubbard

Treadling Variations

Simple Repeat

As with traditional Summer & Winter, there are several different ways to combine the two pattern rows. The first is the "simple repeat," detailed in *Figure 4-3A*. Pattern Row 1 is treadled once, pattern Row 2 is treadled once, and the sequence is repeated. Each pattern row is followed by a selvedge-to-selvedge ground row, alternating treadling between harnesses 1&3 and 2&4. *Photo 4-2* shows a freeform Summer & Winter sampler woven with a simple repeat.

Ph. 4-2. Freeform Summer & Winter simple repeat.

Double Repeat

The second order in which the pattern rows can be woven is called "double repeat". In pattern Row 1, lift harness 1 for weft-faced areas, and change the treadling, lifting harnesses 1,2&4 in warp-faced areas. Repeat this pattern row for a second time. This is followed by pattern Row 2 which is also woven twice, alternating harness 3 in weft-faced areas with harnesses 2,3&4 in warp-faced areas. (Remember to weave a ground row selvedge-to-selvedge after *every* pattern row.)

There are two interesting weave structure variations with the double repeat in Summer & Winter. These variations occur in traditional Summer & Winter as well as the freeform design technique. The ground row which precedes the first row of the double repeat influences the appearance of the pattern: "brick" or "lattice". The "brick" effect occurs when the treadling for the ground weft preceding the first pattern row is harnesses 2&4. *(Photo 4-3)*. The "lattice" effect occurs when treadling for the ground weft preceding the first pattern row is harnesses 1&3. *(Photo 4-4)*.

Ph. 4-3. Freeform Summer & Winter double repeat "brick" (above).

Ph. 4-4. Freeform Summer & Winter double repeat "lattice" (right).

What Color for the Weft?

The decision about color when choosing warp yarns is often easier than the decision about the weft. In fact, the weft may be an after-thought, especially when concentrating on the development of stripes in the warp or blending several shades of one color. For best results, the weft yarns should be selected as the warp is planned.

The weft yarn may be one of the colors used for the warp. In this case, the warp stripe matching the weft color will predominate, since it appears as a solid stripe. Other colors in the warp which approach the weft in value will also appear as solid stripes and predominate.

Avoid the strong temptation to use white, black, or grey or brown unless the color exists in the warp, or unless the specific effect of the neutral color is desired. White weft mutes the colors used in the warp; black intensifies them. Grey and brown tend to wash out the warp colors.

If colors used in the warp are of the same value as one another, a weft in a color between the two may be effective. Also consider the use of the complement of one of the colors. In general, weft yarns which are the same value as the warp visually blend with the warp, whereas weft yarns lighter or darker than the warp are seen as additives to the warp colors.

Figures 4-4A&B gives the Table of Harness Combinations and Treadling for the four pattern rows and four ground rows of the "brick" and "lattice" double repeat.

Try Different Weft Yarns

The following method is helpful for determining the effect of a particular weft yarn upon a given warp before the warp is wound. Wind individual warp yarns around two or three pieces of stiff cardboard, each 4x6". Use each of the colors to be included in the warp for each card, creating the same ratio of colors as in the warp, and using the same number of ends per inch as the sett for the warp. Make the "warp" about 3" wide.

Thread a yard length of weft yarn through a large-eye needle, and needle weave the desired weave

Row:	Harness Combinations:
1	2 + 4
2	1 ← OR → 1,2,4
3	1 + 3
4	1 ← OR → 1,2,4
5	2 + 4
6	3 ← OR → 2,3,4
7	1 + 3
8	3 ← OR → 2,3,4
	weft-faced — ground — warp-faced
	Brick

Row:	Harness Combinations:
1	1 + 3
2	1 ← OR → 1,2,4
3	2 + 4
4	1 ← OR → 1,2,4
5	1 + 3
6	3 ← OR → 2,3,4
7	2 + 4
8	3 ← OR → 2,3,4
	weft-faced — ground — warp-faced
	Lattice

Fig. 4-4 A. Freeform Summer & Winter double repeat "brick".

Fig. 4-4 B. Freeform Summer & Winter double repeat "lattice".

structure. Use a fork to create the desired number of rows per inch. When approximately 2" has been woven, it should be easy to see the effect of the weft yarn with the warp. Repeat this process using different sizes and colors of weft, as well as different weave structures. Save and file these test cards once the weft yarn has been selected.

The Golden Mean

The golden mean is a proportionate ratio of parts to the whole. The proportion is 1:1.618, or 1:1.6. This ratio exists in many aspects of nature and can be readily observed. Each row of spines of a pine cone is 1.6 times the size of the next smaller. Sun flowers have concentric circles, each in a 1:1.6 ratio to those adjacent. The spiral sea shell develops with each spiral larger than the last by a ration of 1:1.6.

The golden mean works equally well for the weaver! Woven pieces are often rectangular. If the top and bottom of a piece are the smaller dimension ("1"), the sides of the piece should be 1.6 times that length to create the most pleasing proportion. If the top and bottom of a piece are 10" (the "1" of the ratio), the length of the longer sides is found by multiplying 10 x 1.6. The answer is 16". If the longer dimension (the "1.6" of the ratio) is known to be 16", then the length of the shorter side is found by dividing 16 by 1.6. The answer is 10". Wallhangings are the most obvious application of the ratio. Other woven items which can utilize the golden mean include accessories, such as handbags and totes, placemats, pillows and rugs.

Consider the amount of area covered by the pattern in Ms & Os or Summer & Winter. If the weft pattern covers roughly one-third or two-thirds of the piece, the result will appear balanced.

The ratio of colors in a piece has already been presented in IN-SIGHTS, on page 39. The main

Single Repeat

A third variation is "single repeat" in which only pattern Row 1 or pattern Row 2 is used throughout the piece. Again, each pattern row is followed by a selvedge-to-selvedge ground row, alternating between harnesses 1&3 and 2&4. The single pattern variation results in a modern linear effect. *Photo 4-5* shows a piece woven in this manner.

Ph. 4-5. Freeform Summer & Winter with single repeat (right).

Freeform Summer & Winter Combined with Twill

It is possible to combine freeform Summer & Winter with straight twill, since each is threaded on harnesses 1,2,3,4. *Figures 4-5A&B* detail freeform Summer & Winter combined with a straight twill. *Photo 4-6* shows an example of a piece woven in this manner.

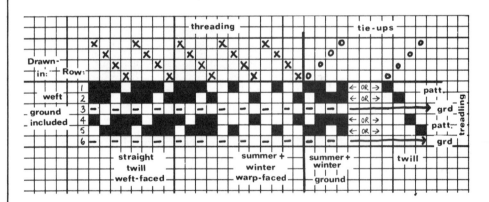

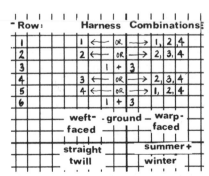

Freeform Summer & Winter combined with straight twill.

Fig. 4-5A. Draw-down (above).

Fig. 4-5B. Table of Harness Combinations and Treadling (left).

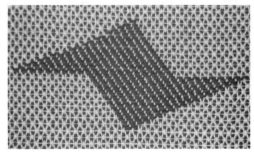

Ph. 4-6. (Right).

Figures 4-6A&B detail Summer & Winter combined with a broken twill, and *Photo 4-7* shows a woven example.

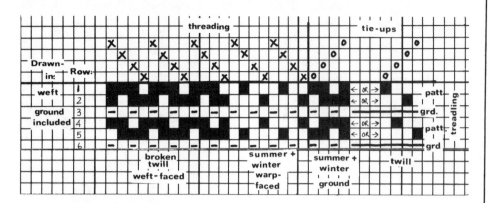

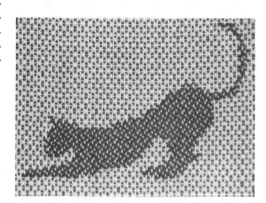

Ph. 4-7. *(Right).*

Freeform Summer & Winter combined with broken twill.

Fig. 4-6A. Draw-down (above).

Fig. 4-6B. Table of Harness Combinations and Treadling (left).

As with freeform twill, the straight twill is more appropriate for designs involving straight lines, and the broken twill is particularly suited to designs involving curved lines.

The Summer & Winter areas of the draw-downs detailed in *Figures 4-5A&B* and *4-6A&B* are woven as a warp-faced weave structure alternating between harness combinations 1,2&4 and 2,3&4. Each Summer & Winter harness combination is repeated twice in both samples (double repeat).

Note that *two* pattern rows are woven before a ground shot is thrown, and that only ground harness combination 1&3 is used. Since both warp-faced harness combinations of the Summer & Winter weave structure include harnesses 2 and 4, the ground row lifting harnesses 2&4 actually does not provide a tie-down for those warp-faced areas. Omitting this one ground row results in an equal compacting of both the Summer & Winter and twill weave structures.

Areas of a weave in which no treadling changes occur within the rows are woven in the same manner for all freeform Summer & Winter techniques. Either the warp- or weft-faced harness combinations of pattern Rows 1 and 2 (or Rows 1 through 4 for Summer & Winter combined with twill) are treadled selvedge-to-selvedge,

color should appear in approximately two-thirds of the piece; the secondary one-third. The ratio is that of the golden mean.

Reverse Side of Piece

When Summer & Winter and broken twill are combined, the ground rows will form into pairs on the backside of the weft-faced broken twill area. This cannot be avoided, but does not detract from the face of the weave.

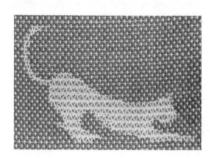

Reverse side of piece woven in freeform Summer & Winter combined with broken twill.

Fool the Eye

If it appears that it will be difficult to maintain smooth edges when weaving a design, select warp and weft yarns which are close to one another in color value. The edge and background of the design will blend slightly and the eye will perceive a smooth edge.

Planning the Geometric Design

Design a geometric motif on graph paper, rather than on lined or plain paper. The squares make it easier to draw horizontal and vertical lines, and to keep the proportions of the motif correct.

Use this graph paper when weaving the motif, rather than a cartoon. Equate each square on the graph paper to a certain number of warp ends or weft rows. If the weaving is large, each square can be scaled to a certain number of inches.

Sleying — A Design Effect

A warp is generally sleyed to result in even spacing of the warp ends. It is possible, however, to create interesting vertical lines in fabric by purposely altering the denting of the warp. If the warp is to be sleyed at 24 epi in a 12 dent reed, the usual method is to sley 2 warp ends per dent. If a warp stripe is desired, the sleying might be: 3,3, 1,1, and repeat. Warp stripes will be created where three warp ends are sleyed in a dent, and a less dense area will occur where one warp end is sleyed. These subtle warp stripes remain once the fabric is washed.

Test Yarns For Shrinkage

It is a good idea to test the amount of shrinkage inherent in a yarn before weaving yardage. This becomes necessary when different yarns are to be combined in warp or weft. To test the amount of shrinkage for a yarn, cut a yard length of each yarn to be tested. Wet these yarns, one at a time, and place them together in a small pot of tepid water. Bring the water to 180°, and then let it cool to room temperature. Remove the yarns and squeeze the excess water from each one. Let the yarns dry. Measure the length of each under tension to compare shrinkage. If the difference is greater than one inch between any of the yarns, an alternative yarn should be considered for the one most different.

"Nothing but itself can copy it."
Ralph Waldo Emerson

depending on whether the fabric surface is to be woven weft-faced or warp-faced. The pattern rows are treadled according to whichever treadling sequence is being used in the piece. Each pattern row is followed by the appropriate ground weft.

Weft Inlay

Weft inlay yarns are added in the pattern rows of freeform Summer & Winter according to the method described in Chapter 2. The addition of weft inlay is successful with all of the freeform Summer & Winter techniques except for Summer & Winter combined with broken twill, in which the inlay will not totally cover the warp-faced weave structure. The pattern weft yarn is woven first, treadling the appropriate warp-faced harness combination in the areas where weft inlay yarns are to be added. When the pattern shuttle has reached the far selvedge, treadle the appropriate weft-faced harness combination for that row, and lay in the additional weft yarns from the underside of the piece. *Photo 4-8* shows a freeform Summer & Winter piece woven with the addition of weft inlay yarns.

Ph. 4-8. Weft inlay added to free-form Summer & Winter

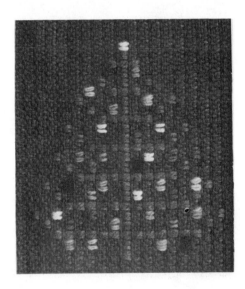

Suitable Projects

As with traditional Summer & Winter, fabrics woven in freeform Summer & Winter are of medium weight, the fabric is firm, and the drape is fair to good. Projects suitable for freeform Summer & Winter include table linens, pillows, accessories, bedspreads, upholstery and decorative embellishments. Refer to Appendix A for details.

(Above)
Ph. 4-9. Set of Christmas cards involving different free-form Summer & Winter techniques.

(Below)
Ph. 4-10. Christmas tree card using double lattice repeat treadling and weft inlay yarns. Woven in 5/2 Verel by the author.

(Above)
Ph. 4-11. Christmas tree card using double brick repeat treadling and weft inlay yarns. Woven in 5/2 Verel by Ann Christensen.

(Right)
Ph. 4-12. Tote bag of 5/2 Verel with double lattice repeat treadling. Woven by Nancy Keegstra.

(Below)
Ph. 4-13. Christmas card of lambs in 40/3 cotton, using double brick repeat treadling. Woven by Mimi Pope.

(Above)
Ph. 4-14. Monogram woven in 5/2 Verel. Woven by Bev Mousseau.

(Left)
Ph. 4-15. Pillow with three designs of cats, woven with simple repeat treadling, using 5/2 Verel. Woven by Nancy Keegstra.

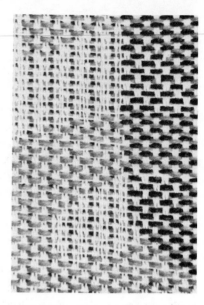

5.

Freeform Ms & Os

Traditional Ms & Os

The traditional Ms & Os weave involves two weave structures not often successfully combined—plain weave and basket weave. The technique however, has withstood the test of time and becomes very interesting when converted from the traditional block weave to freeform design technique.

The two weave structures of traditional Ms & Os differ considerably from one another. One weave structure is plain weave woven over one thread, under one thread, while the second resembles a basket weave and is woven over four threads, under four threads. The basket weave structure (or *extended plain weave*, as I prefer to call it) compacts when woven and resembles an "m", while the plain weave rounds out, resembling an "o", hence the name "Ms & Os". A draw-down for traditional Ms & Os with a sketch showing the weft distortion of the extended plain weave area are detailed in *Figures 5-1A&B. Photo 5-1* shows a portion of a placemat woven in traditional Ms & Os.

Fig. 5-1A. Sketch of weave distortion in traditional Ms & Os.

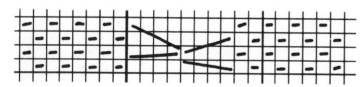

60

Traditional Ms & Os, Bronson and Huck

Ms & Os, huck, and bronson are traditional single-shuttle block weaves which have much in common. They are light weight weaves commonly used for table linens, blankets, draperies and clothing. Each developed originally as a variation of plain weave, and all include plain weave as one of the two weave structures.

In all three weaves, the second weave structure involves warp and/or weft floats. The Ms & Os weave utilizes only weft floats, which appear on both surfaces of the fabric. Huck and bronson may involve warp floats, weft floats or a combination of the two on the weave surface. The underside of the fabric involves floats the opposite of those on the top surface.

The plain and float weave structures are directly reversible in all three techniques. Each weave structure appears in the same areas on both sides of the fabric.

In each weave, it is the effect of the weave structure itself which is attractive. For this reason, the most satisfactory results are obtained by using the same light-colored fine yarns for warp and weft. The use of different colors or textures in the yarns can make it impossible to see the lace.

Treadled As-Drawn-In... by Blocks

The technique of treadling as-drawn-in by blocks is frequently used with overshot as well as other four-block weaves. The result is always pleasing. For an explanation of the basic concept of treadling as-drawn-in and the thread-by-thread method. Refer to INSIGHTS on page 28.

In overshot treadled as-drawn-in by blocks, two harnesses are assigned to each harness combination, and threading and treadling are considered according to blocks of warp threads and blocks of rows.

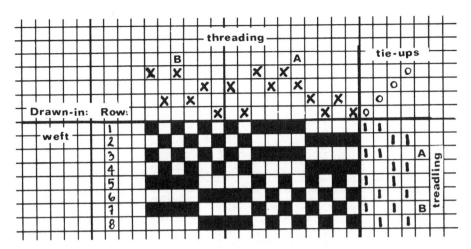

Fig. 5-1B. Draw-down of traditional Ms & Os (above).

Ph. 5-1. Traditional Ms & Os (right).

Freeform Ms & Os

Single Pattern Weft

If just Block "A" (or Block "B") of traditional Ms & Os is repeated selvedge-to-selvedge, harness combinations are possible which will produce both weave structures, plain weave and extended plain weave. *Figure 5-2* shows freeform Ms & Os with Block "A" repeated selvedge-to-selvedge.

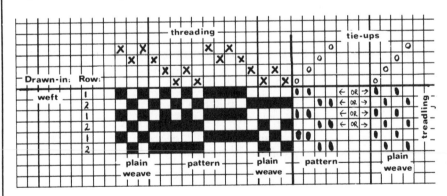

Fig. 5-2. Freeform Ms and Os.

If a piece is woven in freeform Ms & Os with one area in plain weave and the other in extended plain weave, can you imagine what will happen to the area woven in extended plain weave? As with traditional Ms & Os, this extended plain weave area compacts and, in this case, actually distorts the piece. It becomes a very unstable weave. Therefore, it is necessary to add a ground (tabby) row after every pattern row for stability. Additional changes have been made in the harness combinations for better design contrast. The extended plain weave area has been made weft-faced and the plain weave area warp-faced. *Figures 5-3A&B* show freeform Ms & Os as it has been modified; *Photo 5-2* shows both the original and the modified freeform Ms & Os.

Fig. 5-3A. Modified freeform Ms & Os.

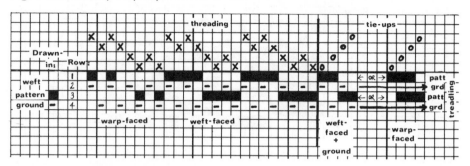

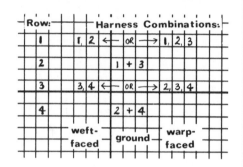

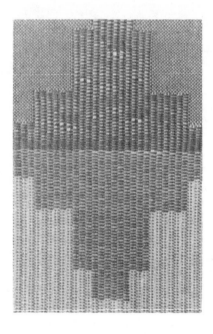

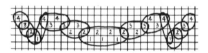

Fig. 5-3B. Table of Harness Combinations and Treadling (above).

Ph. 5-2. Freeform Ms & Os with original treadling shown in the top half of the photo; modified in the lower half.

Freeform Ms & Os is now a weave requiring two wefts; a ground weft of warp size and color, and a pattern weft of a yarn two times the size of the warp and in a contrasting color.

The treadling for each row of pattern weft alternates between the appropriate pair of warp- and weft-faced harness combinations given in *Figure 5-3B.* In pattern Row 1, lift harnesses 1&2 for a weft-faced area. When the pattern is warp-faced, change the treadling and lift harnesses 1,2&3. Alternate the treadling between these two harness combinations as often as the design dictates. A ground row is thrown following Row 1, lifting harnesses 1&3.

In pattern Row 2, for areas to be woven weft-faced, lift harnesses 3&4. For the areas to be woven warp-faced, the treadling is changed to lift harnesses 2,3&4. The treadling for pattern Row 2 alternates between these two harness combinations to accommodate the design. Following Row 2, a ground weft is thrown lifting harnesses 2&4.

With the addition of the ground weft in freeform Ms & Os, the pattern rows are held apart and the warp is very much a part of the design. It is important, therefore, to consider the co-ordination of color between warp and pattern weft. The warp and ground weft

The Key for overshot treadling as-drawn-in by blocks is as follows:

Harnesses		
1&2	—	3&4 Harness Combination
" 2&3	—	4&1 "
" 3&4	—	1&2 "
" 4&1	—	2&3 "

Notice that each harness combination in the Key involves harnesses opposite those of the threading group with which it is paired. Pattern weft is the dominant design factor when weaving overshot. Therefore, the emphasis is on the warp threads which are not lifted on a rising shed loom and are covered by the pattern weft. For instance, if pattern weft is to show over harnesses 1&2, it is necessary to lift harnesses 3&4.

Now look at the threading for honeysuckle overshot.

Honeysuckle overshot threading

The threading blocks are circled, and each block overlaps those adjacent by one thread. Treadling starts with the first circled threading block at the right of the threading. The number of times which the appropriate treadling is repeated depends on the number of threads in that threading block. To square each threading block, the appropriate harness combination is treadled one time less than there are warp threads in the threading block.

Start with the threading block on the far right of the honeysuckle threading, harnesses 3&4. According to the Key, the appropriate treadling for harnesses 3&4 is harness combination 1&2. There are two threads in this threading block, which means that harnesses 1&2 will be treadled two times minus one, or one time.

The next threading block from the right is harnesses 2&3, which means lifting harnesses 4&1 for one row (there are two threads in the threading block). The next threading blocks, consisting of harnesses

1&2 and 4&1, will lift harness combinations 3&4, and 2&3 respectively, each treadled one time.

The next threading block is harnesses 4,3,4,3 which means lifting harnesses 1&2 for three rows (there are four threads in the threading block). This is followed by the threading block of harnesses 3,2,3,2 which means lifting harnesses 4&1 for three rows. The center threading block is harnesses 2,1,2,1,2,1,2. This block is developed by treadling harness combination 3&4 for six pattern rows. The remainder of the treadling sequence is the reverse of the first half.

Because each threading block is woven to square, a woven piece should be square when all threading blocks have been treadled selvedge-to-selvedge. A diagonal line will be evident in the finished piece, traveling from one corner to the other.

An overshot square treadled as-drawn-in by blocks, with the diagonal line emphasized.

are usually the same yarn and will be assumed to be the same in the following examples.

Ph. 5-3. Freeform Ms & Os.

One successful color combination, not often considered, involves warp and pattern weft which are complements (hues opposite one another on the color wheel), but which are close to one another in value, i.e.: medium orange-red warp and medium blue pattern weft. Another successful combination involves analogous hues of differing values, i.e.: light orange warp and maroon pattern weft. A further definition of color terms is presented in INSIGHTS on page 40.

Photo 5-3 is of a piece woven in freeform Ms & Os. While the colors cannot be seen, the value of dark warp and light pattern weft can be easily identified. The warp and ground weft are of a dark reddish brown, a color which co-ordinates well with the light beige and analogous orange pattern wefts.

Two Pattern Wefts

It is possible with freeform Ms & Os to use two separate selvedge-to-selvedge pattern weft yarns simultaneously, creating two different design areas without distorting the weave structure. This very pleasing effect is unique to freeform Ms & Os.

The harness combinations and treadling sequence are presented for this two-pattern Ms & Os in Figure 5-4.

Fig. 5-4A. Freeform Ms & Os with two pattern wefts (below).

Fig. 5-4B. Table of Harness Combinations and Treadling (right).

Row:	weft color:	Harness Combinations:		
1	A	1, 2 ← or →	1, 2, 3	
2	B	3, 4 ← or →	2, 3, 4	
3			2 + 4	
4	A	3, 4 ← or →	2, 3, 4	
5	B	1, 2 ← or →	1, 2, 3	
6			1 + 3	
		weft-faced	ground	warp-faced

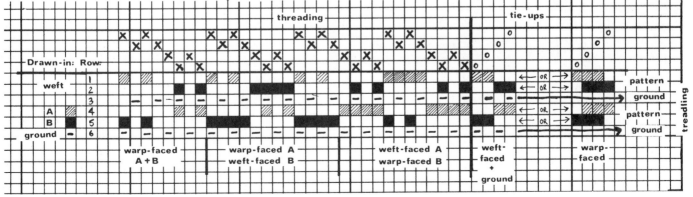

The harness combinations and the treadling sequences for free-form Ms & Os woven with two pattern wefts are basically the same as freeform Ms & Os woven with a single pattern weft. Notice with the technique using two pattern wefts that the two pattern shuttles alternate, and a ground row is woven after every pair of pattern weft rows.

To be most effective, the designs developed with each of these pattern weft yarns should be in different areas of the piece, although they may overlap. Again, it is important to consider the value and color choice for warp and weft. The warp (and ground weft) and two pattern weft yarns can be of differing hues which are close in value, i.e.: gold warp (and ground weft), medium blue and light rust pattern wefts. Another choice is analogous hues of differing values, i.e.: yellow warp, deep reddish brown and orange pattern wefts. *Photo 5-4* shows a piece woven with two pattern wefts using the above combination of analogous hues.

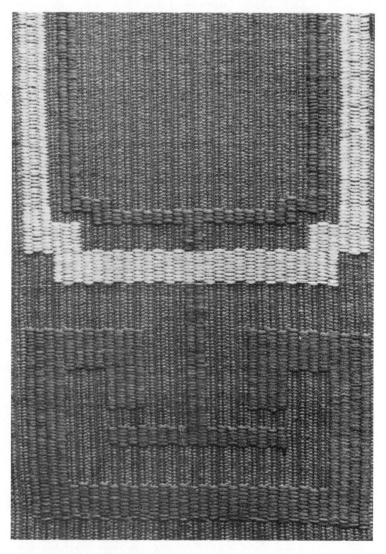

Ph. 5-4. Freeform Ms & Os
with two pattern wefts. An
enlargement of a jacket front,
in which the warp and ground
weft are navy blue; the
pattern weft yarns, yellow
and rust.

The Order of Ground Rows

Many weaves involve the use of two weft shuttles, one of which is a ground weft. Because the pattern weft covers the ground weft almost entirely, it may be difficult to remember which ground harness combination should be treadled next. A hint follows which should help keep the treadling order of the ground weft rows straight. Start both the ground and pattern shuttles at the same selvedge, and weave the pattern weft shuttle first. If the two shuttles come from the left selvedge, the appropriate ground harness combination is 2&4. If the two shuttles are at the right selvedge, the appropriate ground harness combination is 1&3. In short, shuttles on the left, lift harnesses 2&4 for ground; shuttles on the right, lift harnesses 1&3 for ground.

Counterbalance Treadling

If you weave on a counterbalance loom, there should be no difficulty adapting rising shed instructions. If harnesses are lifted on the rising shed loom (harnesses 1&2), it is necessary to activate the opposite harnesses on a counterbalance loom to obtain the same shed (harnesses 3&4).

If the counterbalance weaver understands that the pattern is developed with the reverse side of the weaving up, it may not be necessary to reverse the treadling. The piece simply must be turned over when it is taken off the loom to have the "right side up".

"Idleness is the only real sin. A blacksmith singing at his forge, sparks aflying, anvil ringing, the man materializing an idea—what is finer?"

Elbert Hubbard

In areas of a piece requiring no treadling changes within each row, the appropriate warp- or weft-faced harness combinations are treadled selvedge-to-selvedge. The ground weft is woven as usual after one or two pattern weft rows, depending on the technique being woven.

Weft Inlay

To add weft inlay yarns, the pattern weft shuttle is woven first, and is treadled for the warp-faced harness combination in areas where weft inlay yarns are to be added. The appropriate weft-faced harness combination for that row is treadled, and the weft yarns are laid in from the underside of the weaving as described in Chapter 2. If two pattern weft yarns are used, both pattern weft yarns are woven before the weft inlay yarns are added.

Suitable Projects

Freeform Ms & Os finishes in a somewhat heavier weave than the other techniques presented thus far. In fact, it is the only technique of the lighter weight freeform weaves which is also suitable for rugs. Freeform Ms & Os results in a firm fabric with fair to good drape. Other applications of this weave include heavier table linens, outer wear, accessories, upholstery, pillows and wallhangings. Refer to Appendix A for details.

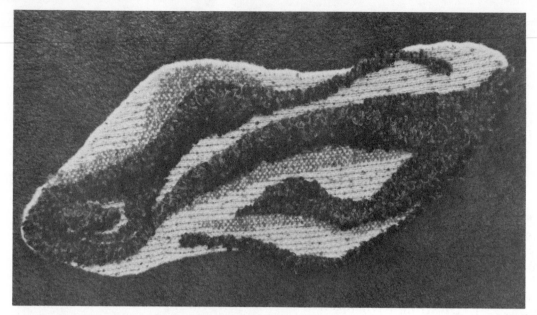

(Left)
Ph. 5-5. Shaped rug of medium weight wool and 10/2 linen with two pattern wefts. The weft floats are pulled up into loops for textural effect. Woven by the author.

(Right center)
Ph. 5-6. Enlargement of an area of the shaped rug.

(Above)
Ph. 5-7. Heavy coat involving two pattern wefts, using 3/12 and 20/2 wool. Woven by the author.

(Right)
Ph. 5-8. Framed wallhanging in medium weight wool and 5/2 cotton, with a single pattern weft. Woven by Barbara Swietlik.

(Right)
Ph. 5-9. Placemats with a single pattern weft. Woven in 5/2 Verel by Linda Rockwell.

(Below)
Ph. 5-10. Enlargement of an area of one placemat.

(Below)
Ph. 5-11. Framed hanging in 10/2 linen and medium weight wool, involving two pattern wefts. Woven by Peggy MacArthur.

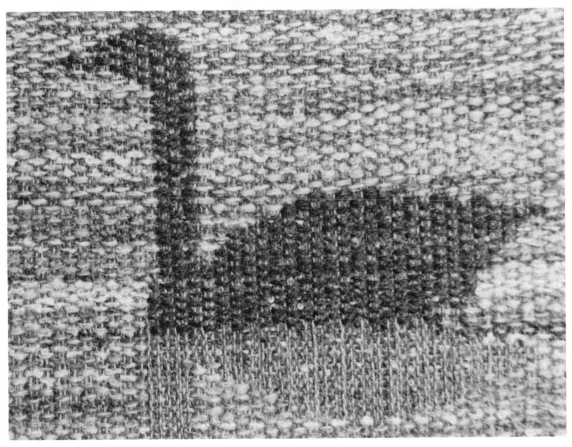

6.

Freeform Huck

Traditional Huck

Traditional four-harness huck, a weave structure involving blocks of either warp or weft floats and plain weave, converts nicely to a freeform design technique. There may be one, two, or three threads forming the warp or weft floats in one threading or treadling sequence. *Figure 6-1* details the draw-down for traditional huck woven with single warp and weft floats. An example of traditional huck woven with a single warp float is shown in *Photo 6-1*.

Fig. 6-1. Traditional huck with single floats.

(Figure 6-1: weaving draft draw-down grid. Labels include: "plain weave", "threading", "tie-ups", "B A B A", "Drawn-in:", "Row:", "warp", "warp floats", "weft", "weft floats", "treadling", "B A A B", "ground", "plain weave", "lace", Row numbers 1–14.)

INSIGHTS

The Huck Weave

It is thought that the weave structure bearing the name "huck" was not in use in this country prior to the mid 1800s. The technique was used widely in England and, possibly, Scotland prior to that time, but had not been introduced to the American weaver. The traditional weave is used most often for table linens, using fine cotton or linen yarns. Huck toweling is used today as a ground fabric for swedish embroidery and other forms of embroidery and needle-weaving. The weave structure of huck is appropriate as a ground fabric because the floats do not overlap as they do in bronson. The floats therefore provide a firm, symmetrically organized ground upon which to work embroidery stitches.

68

The Heritage of Freeform Huck

The technique presented in this chapter as "freeform huck" appears as a multiple-harness block weave or 4-harness pick-up technique in Scandinavian countries. One translation for the name of this weave is "Diversified Plain Weave". The technique is most often woven using fine yarns and symmetrical designs. The woven fabric is used primarily for linens.

Similar Warp and Weft Density in Freeform Huck

If similar density is desired in the warp- and weft-faced areas of freeform huck, double the heavy warp yarn, counting two heavy warp ends as one. This is usually feasible without changing the sett. The use of a light weight pattern weft yarn is also possible. The following Photo shows a small sample in which the heavy warp is 5/2 cotton. The warp is threaded singly on the sides of the piece, and is doubled in the center. The entire warp is sleyed at 30 ends per inch.

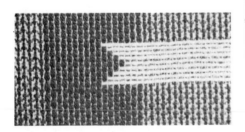

Sample showing two warp densities.

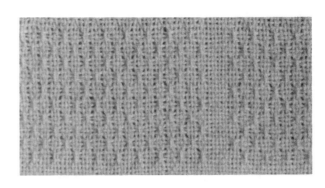

Ph. 6-1. Traditional single warp floats.

Freeform Huck

The threading unit to be repeated selvedge-to-selvedge for freeform huck consists of one sequence each of the two traditional threadings. Harness combinations can be devised which will create either the weft float or warp float weave structures as well as plain weave. Thus, the basic requirements for conversion to freeform design technique have been satisfied.

Photos 6-2 and 6-3 show a piece woven in freeform huck. While the weave structures are the same for freeform and traditional huck, it is doubtful that the piece would be identified immediately as woven in huck! The draw-down for freeform huck is detailed in Figure 6-2A, and the Table of Harness Combinations and Treadling in Figure 6-2B.

Ph. 6-2. A sampler woven in freeform huck.
Ph. 6-3. Detail of Photo 6-2.

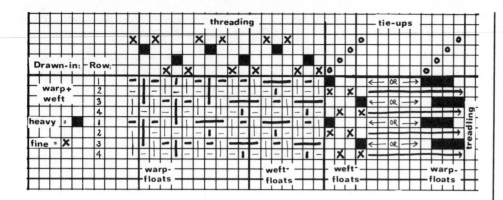

Freeform huck.

Fig. 6-2A. Draw-down (top).

Fig. 6-2B. Table of Harness Combinations and Treadling (bottom).

The intriguing nature of this weave is created by the size and color of both warp and weft yarns. In the threading, warp ends threaded on harnesses 1 and 4 are of a fine weight yarn, and are the tie-down threads. The warp yarns which form the pattern warp floats are threaded on harnesses 2 and 3. They are of a heavy yarn three to four times the size of the fine warp and in a contrasting color. If the fine warp is 20/2 cotton, then the heavy warp should be 5/2 cotton. If the fine warp is 5/2 cotton, then the heavy warp should be a medium weight rug yarn.

It is usually possible to wind and beam the fine and heavy warps together. However, if the two yarns have distinctly different stretch properties, then it may be necessary to wind the two warps separately and double beam them.

If the heavy and fine warps are wound and beamed together, the method of winding the two must be modified slightly so as to have the correct number of heavy and fine warp ends for each threading sequence. There are six warp ends in one threading sequence, four fine and two heavy. Wind the fine and heavy together for a total of four warp ends, and then wind two more of just the fine. When threading, only one fine warp end will be out of order in each repeat of the 6-end sequence. This warp end can be removed from the cross and placed where needed as each sequence is threaded.

Because two different yarns are being used, determining the sett for freeform huck may seem a bit confusing at first. Figure the sett which will square the weave for the heavy warp. If the heavy warp is 5/2 cotton, the sett to square is 15 ends per inch. Double that number to find the total number of ends needed per inch for freeform huck. Using 5/2 cotton as the heavy warp yarn, 30 epi are necessary to accommodate both the heavy and fine warps. Using a 15 dent reed, sley two ends per dent.

Freeform Huck Edges

The warp for freeform huck involves the use of both fine and heavy yarns. Because the heavy yarn is the more prominent, it is best to thread a heavy warp end at either edge of the piece. With an even number of fine and heavy yarns, one edge warp end will be heavy, while the other will be fine. Simply lay back the outside fine warp end.

Freeform Huck Woven "Conventionally"

It is possible to convert traditional huck to a freeform technique. However, the weave tends to look sparse, and fabric depends upon weft inlay for visual interest as the floats do not overlap. Therefore, the technique is not presented with the more versatile variation of freeform huck detailed in Chapter 6.

One example of freeform huck, as it was conventionally developed, does appear in the Preface and again on page 75. This is a small framed woven painting. Notice the warp floats and weft floats which form the design. Much of the area involving weft floats has been developed using weft inlay yarns. The piece shown was originally a sample for a larger one. Because of the time necessary to finish this smaller one, it became the final product!

"Don't part with your illusions. When they are gone you may still exist, but you have ceased to live."

Mark Twain

Adding Color in Freeform Huck

With freeform huck, pleasing effects are possible by working with color changes in the warp or weft. The heavy or fine yarns of the warp or weft can involve subtle striping. It is most effective when either the warp OR the weft involves several colors. Shading or striping in both warp and weft must be handled carefully to prevent visual confusion. The following Photo shows a freeform huck piece woven with subtle shading of blues and purples in the heavy warp and a solid orange heavy weft. The fine yarns are orange for the warp and blue for the weft.

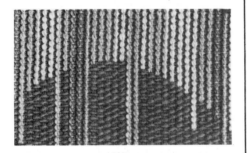

Warp shading in freeform huck.

Cut! Do Not Unweave

When an error is discovered which has been made several inches back in the weaving, and which must be corrected, there are two approaches. The more common approach is to "unweave" those several inches. This is necessary if the weft yarn being used is in limited supply. If at all possible, however, it is much faster, particularly with freeform design techniques, to cut your weft rows and pull them out. With the warp under tension, separate the warp ends at the center to expose the weft rows. Then cut through the weft rows between the separated warp ends, being very careful not

Two weft yarns are necessary for weaving freeform huck, one the weight of the fine warp and the other the weight of the heavy warp. The colors, however, are reversed from the warp. For example, if the heavy pattern warp is red and the fine tie-down warp is white, then the heavy pattern weft is white, and the fine tie-down weft red. The design areas woven with warp floats (warp-faced) are developed by the heavy red warp. The areas woven with weft floats (weft-faced) are developed by the heavy white weft.

In Row 1, the heavy weft is used. For design areas which are to be woven with weft floats, lift harness 1. When the design calls for warp floats, the treadling is changed to lift harnesses 1,2&3. As the shuttle moves through the shed, the treadling can be changed from one harness combination to the other within that row as many times as the design dictates.

Row 2 is a ground row in which the fine weft is thrown selvedge-to-selvedge lifting harnesses 1&3.

Weave Row 3 in the same manner as Row 1. Areas to be woven with weft floats lift harness 4. For areas to be woven with warp floats change the treadling and lift harnesses 2,3&4. Once again, the treadling alternates between the two harness combinations according to the design.

Row 4 is a ground row woven selvedge-to-selvedge with the fine weft lifting harnesses 2&4.

Notice that fine and heavy weft yarns alternate in the treadling, whereas two fine yarns follow each heavy yarn in the warp. This departure from the expected order of identical yarn sequence of warp and weft prevents the warp floats from becoming too long.

Because of the difference between the warp and weft yarn sequence, the weft-faced areas will appear more compact than the warp-faced areas. There are more heavy weft rows per inch than heavy warp ends. This difference enhances a piece, rather than detracting from it.

In an area of a piece woven without any treadling changes, the heavy weft is thrown selvedge-to-selvedge lifting the appropriate warp- or weft-faced harness combinations. The fine weft is then thrown selvedge-to-selvedge in the usual fashion, following every pattern row.

Weft Inlay

The addition of weft inlay yarns is a simple matter with freeform huck. The treadling for the heavy weft yarn alternates between the appropriate warp- and weft-faced harness combinations according to the design. Any areas in which inlay yarns are to be added are also treadled warp-faced. Once the pattern weft shuttle has reached the far selvedge, the weft-faced harness combination for that row is treadled, and the weft inlay yarns are placed from the underside according to instructions given in Chapter 2. The fine weft yarn is then thrown selvedge-to-selvedge. *Photos 6-4* and *6-5* show a piece woven with the addition of weft inlay.

Ph. 6-4. *Freeform huck with weft inlay.*

Ph. 6-5. *Enlargement of one area of Photo 6-4.*

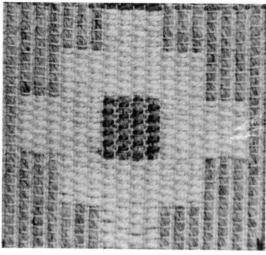

Suitable Projects

Freeform huck results in a fabric which is firm but drapes well. The fabric is successful either as a light weight material using 5/2 and finer cottons (or other yarns of comparable size), or as a heavyweight material using fine rug weight wools and heavier yarns. Because both fine and heavy yarns are used in warp and weft, even the heavy weight fabrics drape well. Freeform huck is best suited for outerwear, accessories, medium weight clothing, table linens, pillows, bedspreads, upholstery and wallhangings. Refer to Appendix A for details.

to cut any warp! Pull the weft rows out from each selvedge edge. If the warp is wide, it may be necessary to make two cuts, dividing the weft into thirds.

Warp separated and scissors ready to cut.

Weave Hems Using a Finer Weft

It is often difficult to avoid an unsightly finish to the hem when weaving a bulky fabric for accessories, table linens, or garments. In many situations, it is possible to weave the hems using a finer weft yarn, thus providing a trim, flat hem. Care must be taken, however, to use a weft yarn with little or no stretch, as the warp tends to pull in more when a fine weft is used.

"Living is a daily experience."
Gary Gruber

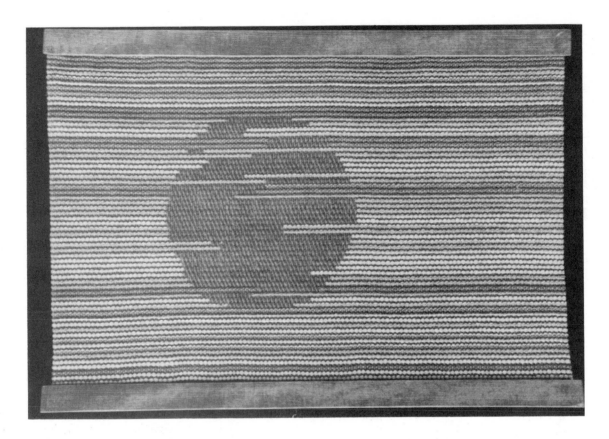

Ph. 6-6. Wallhanging in fine and medium weight wool. An enlargement of this piece appears on the book's cover. Woven by Kathie Roig.

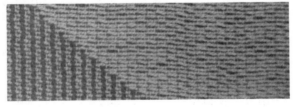

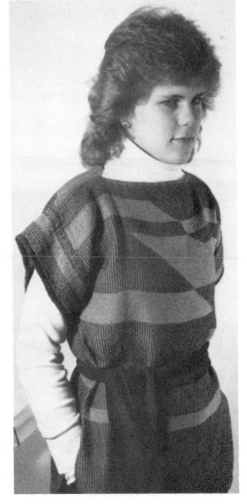

(Right)
Ph. 6-7. Light weight shirt in 5/2 Verel cotton. Woven by Kathie Roig.

(Above)
Ph. 6-8. Enlargement of an area of the shirt in Photo 6-7.

(Above)
Ph. 6-9. Small fine and medium weight wool clutch bag with a panda design motif involving weft inlay yarns. Woven by Mugs O'Toole.

(Right)
Ph. 6-10. Hanging rug of medium and heavy weight wools. Woven by Ann Christensen.

(Above)
Ph. 6-11. Enlargement of an area of the wool rug.

(Below)
Ph. 6-12. "Strip vest" of handspun and dyed wool, finished with a knitted waistband. Woven by Lois Crocker.

(Left)
Ph. 6-13. Heavy jute and cotton belt. Woven by Jo Ann Nelson.

Ph. 6-14. Framed wallhanging of dunes woven in 10/2 linen, using the "conventional" freeform huck. Woven by the author.

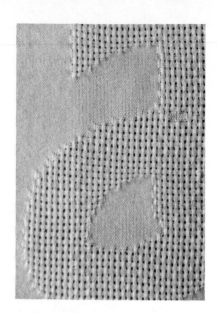

7.

Freeform Lace Huck

Traditional Lace Huck

Traditional lace huck is usually woven with a double float, a five-thread block in both threading and treadling containing two warp or weft floats. Blocks of warp and weft floats are woven simultaneously, alternating within a pattern area. The huck float areas in a piece are complimented by plain weave. Freeform lace huck will also be presented as double float blocks and plain weave. Traditional lace huck is shown in *Figure 7-1* and *Photo 7-1*.

Traditional lace huck.

Ph. 7-1 (right).

Fig. 7-1 (below).

Close Colors For Freeform Lace Huck

When using two different colors or two shades of one color for warp and weft in freeform lace huck, it is imperative that the two colors be close to one another in value. If the colors are too far apart, the lace areas will scarcely show against the striping in the warp and weft.

Test the value of the two yarns by the "barber pole" method. Twist the yarns together. If they show as separate colors and form a twist which resembles a barber pole, the values of the two yarns are not close enough to be used together. Two yarns which are suitably close in value should appear to blend when twisted together.

"Simplicity is the glory of expression."

Walt Whitman

Lace emphasis

It is possible to emphasize each block unit in freeform lace huck by leaving one dent empty following every sequence of five warp ends. The space created by the empty dent results in a subtle warp stripe between lace blocks. This adds a pleasing effect to both lace and plain weave areas.

If 5/2 cotton is sleyed at 15 ends per inch in a 15 dent reed, the ends are sleyed one per dent. In order to leave one dent free following every sequence of five warp ends, it is necessary to sley two ends together within each group. Five warp ends are sleyed in four dents, and the fifth dent is left empty.

An alternate method of denting 15 ends per inch is to use a 12 dent reed. A sequence of five warp ends is sleyed 2,1,2, the next dent is left empty, and the sequence is repeated. In order to accommodate different numbers of ends per inch, some figuring may be necessary to allow an empty dent to follow each sequence of five warp ends. Almost any number of ends per inch can be accommodated by using an 8, 10, 12 or 15 dent reed.

Yarns Best Suited for Freeform Lace Huck and Bronson

Lace huck and bronson are usually woven with a fine yarn of a light color. Warp and weft traditionally are the same yarn. This traditional approach also works best with the freeform lace techniques. The most successful yarns for freeform lace huck and bronson are cotton, silk, non-stretchy wool, and synthetics (modacrylics and other synthetic blends which use acrylic fibers). Because linen has no stretch, it is best not to use this yarn for the freeform technique.

A yarn comparable in size to 5/2 cotton (or finer) results in the most attractive lace effect. When using yarns finer than 10/2 cotton, it is best to select a natural fiber. The shrinkage inherent in natural fibers

Freeform Lace Huck

Threading for freeform lace huck is derived from the traditional threading and consists of one repeat each of the two huck blocks, repeated selvedge-to-selvedge. The two weave structures involved in freeform lace huck, lace and plain weave, are both balanced weaves. These two weave structures can be combined as a freeform design technique because they appear distinctly different from one another. Harness combinations are possible which will weave areas either in lace huck or in plain weave. It can therefore be said that lace huck converts successfully to a freeform design technique. The draw-down (Figure 7-2A) and the Table of Harness Combinations and Treadling (Figure 7-2B) are given for freeform lace huck.

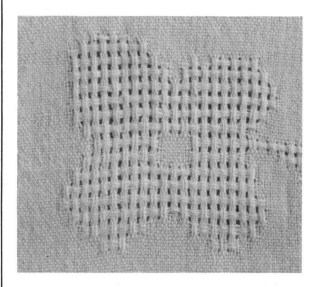

Ph. 7-2. Detail of freeform lace huck baby blanket woven in 5/2 Verel (cotton count).

Fig. 7-2A. Freeform lace huck (below).

Fig. 7-2B. Table of Harness Combinations and Treadling (right).

Row:	Harness Combinations:
1	2,4
2	1, 3 ← OR → 1, 2
3	2,4
4	1, 3 ← OR → 1, 2
5	2,4
6	1, 3
7	2, 4 ← OR → 3, 4
8	1, 3
9	2, 4 ← OR → 3, 4
10	1, 3
	plain weave — lace

In freeform lace huck, only four rows of the total ten involve changes of harness combinations: Rows 2,4,7&9. The shuttle is thrown selvedge-to-selvedge in the remaining six rows: Rows 1,3,5, 6,8,10.

To clarify the method of weaving freeform lace huck, the ten rows given in *Figure 7-2A&B* follow in detail. *Row 1* is treadled selvedge-to-selvedge lifting harnesses 2&4. *Row 2* involves a choice of harness combinations. For plain weave areas, lift harnesses 1&3. For lace areas, the treadling is changed to lift harnesses 1&2. *Row 3* is again treadled selvedge-to-selvedge lifting harnesses 2&4. *Row 4* repeats the choice of harness combinations in Row 2. *Row 5* is treadled selvedge-to-selvedge lifting harnesses 2&4.

Rows 6 through 10 are woven in the same manner as the first five rows, but use different harness combinations. In *Rows 6,8 and 10*, lift harnesses 1&3. In the pattern rows, *Rows 7 and 9*, lift harnesses 2&4 in areas where plain weave is to be woven, and harnesses 3&4 in areas where lace is to be woven.

Notice in *Figure 7-2A* that the vertical design line is changed at one point by weaving one warp float instead of two. It is possible to develop a gradual vertical line movement in this way. Likewise, it is possible to change the horizontal design by one weft float instead of two, also shown in *Figure 7-2A*.

When weaving a single float, it is important to use a warp float for the vertical design line, and a weft float for the horizontal design line. If a vertical line is changed by one-half of a weft float, or a horizontal line by one-half of a warp float, the length of the float is shortened. It is more noticeable when floats are one-half their length than when one float is woven instead of two.

Color Variation For Warp and Weft

One color variation involving both the warp and weft yarns merits attention. This variation applies to traditional lace huck as well as the freeform design technique. To emphasize lace areas, two close shades of the same color, or two colors similar in value, are used in both warp and weft. In the warp, the light shade is threaded on the harnesses which form the lace floats, harnesses 2 and 3. Harnesses 1 and 4 are threaded with the darker color.

When weaving the two-shade warp, the same alternation of color is used in the weft. Rows 1,3,5,6,8 and 10 are treadled using the darker color. The rows which form the lace, Rows 2,4,7 and 9, are treadled using the light shade.

The effects of this two-shade combination are very interesting. The lace area becomes more evident when a slightly lighter shade is used for the floats. A small repeat of the log cabin weave develops in the plain weave area, which adds a pleasing visual dimension. *Photo 7-3* is of a shawl which has been woven using two shades of one color in warp and weft.

As with freeform huck, a slightly different method must be used when winding the warp. There are ten warp ends in each of the treadling sequences, 6 darker and 4 light. To attain the correct number of each color yarn in each threading block, wind one light and one darker warp end together for a total of eight ends. Drop the light color yarn and wind two more single darker ends. This gives a total of ten warp ends in each threading repeat with the correct color

allows the lace design to be better defined. It may be difficult to see the design clearly until the piece has been shrunk, especially when using finer yarns in a piece.

Fixing a Broken Warp Thread

The following method of coping with a broken warp thread results in the replacement of the original warp thread into the warp after a few inches of weaving. This method eliminates the need to reposition and retie a replacement thread throughout the weaving after the warp thread breaks.

A warp thread usually breaks between the weaving edge and the reed as it rests against the harnesses. The following instructions are based on this assumption. 1)Cut a replacement warp thread 1 yard long. 2)Thread one end of the replacement thread through the appropriate dent in the reed and heddle, pulling the back part of the original warp thread out of the reed and heddle as you go. 3)Pull the replacement thread through the reed and heddle until only 3" overlaps the weaving. 4)Secure the front end of the replacement thread and front end of the original warp end (if long enough) around a pin about 1" from the edge of the weaving. 5)At the back beam, tie the replacement thread, in a bow, to the back part of the original warp end. Tie to weaving tension. 6)Weave to a point 3" beyond the break. 7)Untie the bow behind the harnesses. 8) Bring the original warp end forward through the heddle and reed, pulling the replacement thread forward and out of the heddle and reed as you go. 9)Secure the replacement thread and original warp end around a pin, to tension, about 1" from the weaving edge.

Once the weaving is off the loom, and before the piece is washed or ironed, remove the 2 pins which secure the broken end and, using a large eye needle, weave in the two ends at each pin to overlap one another by 1". Clip the ends.

The Density of Selvedge-to-Selvedge Shots vs. Pattern Areas

In most of the techniques presented, areas of a piece in which the shuttles travel selvedge-to-selvedge will compact more closely than areas involving treadling changes within each row. This is due in part to the effects of the treadling changes on the weave structures. Also, one tends to beat somewhat more firmly in areas where the weaving moves along more quickly. If the weaver is aware that the density of the woven fabric may vary, that should be sufficient to prevent the problem.

Design Perspective While Weaving

As a design is being woven, it is easy to become overly critical of its development. Working 15 inches or so from the cloth encourages too close an observation of each row as it is woven. Therefore, it is necessary to view the weaving from a greater distance to see the development of the piece in its true perspective. To observe the piece in its entirety, unroll the cloth beam and allow the fabric to hang over the front beam. Do not look at the piece for several hours. Then return and trust your first impression to be an honest reaction.

"Idleness is the Dead Sea that swallows all virtues: Be active in business, that temptation may miss her aim; the bird that sits is easily shot."
Elbert Hubbard

Ph. 7-3. Enlargement of one area of a shawl woven in two shades of one color in warp and weft.

distribution. When threading each lace block, two warp ends will need to be removed from the cross and placed in sequence. This is much easier, however, than preparing two separate warps and juggling both in the beaming and threading process.

For areas of a piece involving no treadling changes within the rows, the appropriate harness combinations are treadled selvedge-to-selvedge for either plain weave or lace. If lace is to be woven selvedge-to-selvedge, it is necessary to adjust the beat to prevent the lace structure from becoming too compact.

Weft Inlay

Freeform lace huck is the one freeform design technique presented which does not accommodate weft inlay yarns. The addition of inlay yarns to the selvedge-to-selvedge weft distorts the weave rather than enhancing it.

Suitable Projects

Freeform lace huck is a very delicate weave with the potential to resemble bobbin lace when woven with fine yarns. The weave is suitable for table linens, yardage (especially finer fabrics for blouses and light weight skirts and jackets), accessories (such as shawls), light weight throws, wallhangings, and fine lace to use as inserts. Refer to Appendix A for details.

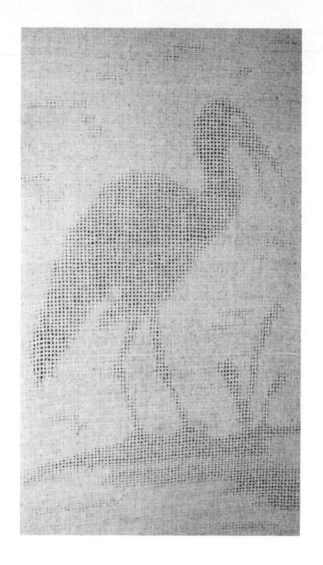

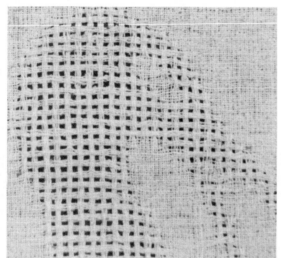

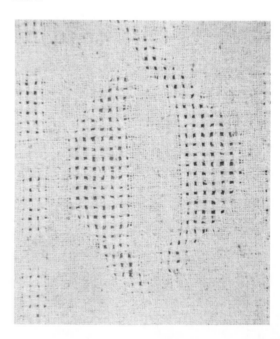

(Above)
Ph. 7-6. Skirt woven in 40/2 tussah silk. By the author.

(Below)
Ph. 7-7. Enlargement of an area of the skirt.

(Above top)
Ph. 7-4. Wallhanging woven in 40/2 silk entitled "Blue Heron". By the author.

(Above)
Ph. 7-5. Enlargement of an area of "Blue Heron".

80

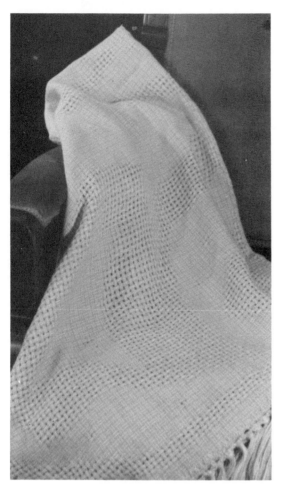

Ph. 7-10. Shawl woven in 5/2 Verel, with two colors in both warp and weft. Woven by the author.

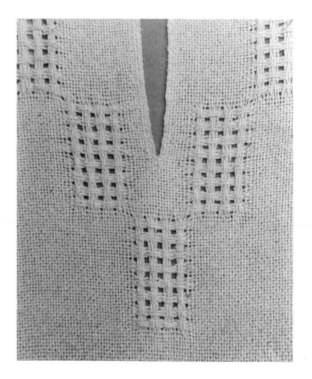

(Above)
Ph. 7-8. Light weight shirt in 5/2 Verel. Woven by Ann Christensen.

(Below)
Ph. 7-9. Enlargement of an area of the shirt in Ph. 7-8.

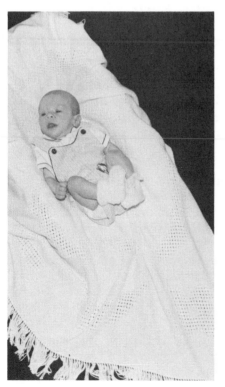

Ph. 7-11. Baby blanket in 5/2 Verel. Woven by the author.

8.

Freeform Bronson Lace

Traditional Bronson Lace

Bronson lace consists of two weave structures. One is plain weave, and the second is lace which is created by warp-floats on the fabric surface and weft-floats simultaneously woven on the underside of the fabric. As with lace huck, each threading and treadling repeat usually involves a double float. There is one tie-down thread between lace units which occurs in both the threading and treadling and forms a small cross between each lace unit. It is this cross or "window", as it is often called, which characterizes bronson lace. A draw-down of traditional bronson lace appears in *Figure 8-1*, and *Photo 8-1* shows the weave structure of bronson lace.

Fig. 8-1. Traditional bronson lace.

INSIGHTS

The Heritage of Bronson

Evidence of what we call "bronson" has been found in historic textile archives of several European countries, and the weave probably dates back several centuries. Because fabrics woven in bronson (and other so-called "linen" weaves) were woven using very fine linen and cotton yarns, it is not surprising that few pieces remain today to document its heritage. As linen or cotton fabrics became old and tattered, they were torn for use in rag rugs. With all of the work put into these fabrics, they were never discarded until all possible use had been derived from them!

In 1817, two brothers with the last name "Bronson" published a book for the American home weaver entitled "The Domestic Manufacturer's Assistant and Family Directory of the Arts of Weaving and Dyeing". In contemporary terms, this was a guide for the home weaver and natural dyer.

This book was used for several decades but was then considered obsolete as the manufacture of textiles became industrialized.

Mary Atwater came across the book in the late 1930s and wished to share the attractive linen weave which appeared in the book, but was not named. In deference to the Bronson brothers and their efforts to educate the home weavers, she named the weave structure "bronson". Later, Mary Atwater encountered the same weave structure in English textile archives under the name "spot weave". The weave still is referred to as "spot weave" or "spot bronson", but the name "bronson" is perhaps more frequently used.

Floating Selvedge

When weaving twill, or any weave other than plain weave, it is difficult to maintain straight edges and consistently catch the edge warp threads with the weft. The floating selvedge, which permits the weaving of plain weave around the edge threads of a weaving, solves both of the above problems.

The floating selvedge consists of a single warp thread on either side of the warp which is handled somewhat differently than the rest of the warp. (If the yarn used for the warp is stretchy or not particularly strong, two warp ends may be used for each floating selvedge.) The threads for the floating selvedges can be the outermost warp thread on either side of the warp which has been beamed.

These two selvedge threads are not threaded through heddles, but are sleyed in the reed with the rest of the warp. Each floating selvedge should be sleyed in a dent by itself, if possible.

The floating selvedge should be placed under slightly greater tension than the rest of the warp. This is most easily accomplished by attaching a weight to each floating selvedge under the warp beam. A sinker for a fishing line can usually be clipped directly to each selvedge

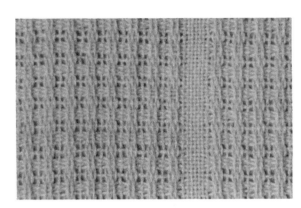

Ph. 8-1. Bronson lace structure.

Freeform Bronson Lace

When converting bronson lace to the freeform technique, the first consideration is the threading. If one block (Block "A") of the traditional lace threading is repeated selvedge-to-selvedge, it is possible to devise harness combinations for both weave structures inherent in bronson lace. *Figure 8-2* details a draw-down of freeform bronson lace with a threading unit of Block "A", harnesses 1,2,1, 2,1,3, repeated selvedge-to-selvedge. It is also possible to convert bronson lace using Block "B" of the traditional weave.

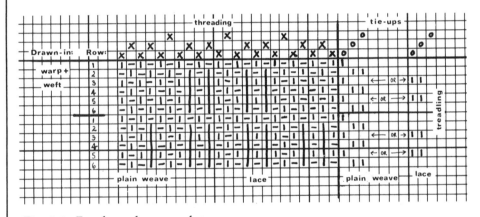

Fig. 8-2. Freeform bronson lace threaded 1,2,1,2,1,3.

While conversion is successful using the Block "A" threading unit, notice that one half of the warp ends are threaded on harness 1, and that harness 4 is not used at all. This is acceptable, but, as with Summer & Winter, it is advisable to seek another threading which distributes the threads more evenly between the harnesses. While it is not possible to distribute the warp ends equally, this threading is successful and will be used for conversion of bronson lace to the freeform technique. *Figure 8-3A* details a draw-down of freeform bronson in which all four harnesses are employed. The Table of Harness Combinations and Treadling is given in *Figure 8-3B*, and an enlargement of an area of a piece woven in freeform bronson is shown in *Photo 8-2*.

As with traditional bronson lace, one weft yarn the color and size of the warp yarn is used. Six rows are necessary to complete one treadling sequence, and only Rows 3 and 5 involve treadling changes to form the lace areas. The remaining rows (1,2,4&6) are woven selvedge-to-selvedge.

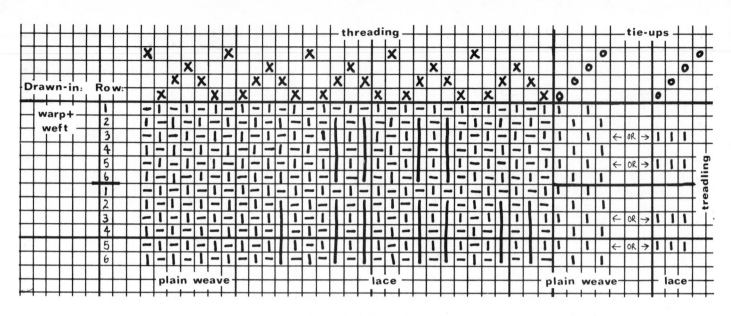

Fig. 8-3A. Freeform bronson lace threaded 1,2,3,2,1,4. (above)

Fig. 8-3B. Table of Harness Combinations and Treadling (right)

Row:	Harness Combinations and Treadling:		
1	1,3		
2	2,4		
3	1,3 ← or → 1,2,3		
4	2,4		
5	1,3 ← or → 1,2,3		
6	2,4		
	plain weave — lace		

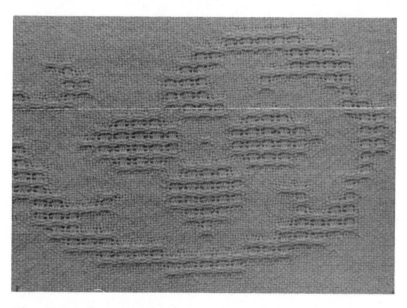

Ph. 8-2. Freeform bronson lace.

thread and works very well. A few washers attached to a paper clip, which, in turn, is clipped to the selvedge thread, works equally as well. The weight should be only what is necessary to add slight tension to the floating selvedges. Too much weight may actually distort the weaving, or break the selvedge thread.

When prepared, the floating selvedges should sit slightly above the warp, and rest halfway between the top and bottom warp of a shed when a harness combination is activated. If they are too low, it may be necessary to tie them to the proper height from behind the harnesses by tying them up to the top castle (the supporting frame for the harnesses).

The shuttle enters each shed over the floating selvedge and exists the shed under the floating selvedge. Every row is the same: enter over, exit under. It is this consistent attention to the outside warp end that provides the plain weave structure around that thread.

One word of caution: when you stop weaving, even for an hour, it is best to remove the weights from the selvedge threads, or bring the weights up to rest on the back beam. This will prevent the warp threads from stretching and weakening.

According to *Figure 8-3A&B*, Rows 1&2 are woven selvedge-to-selvedge lifting harnesses 1&3, 2&4 respectively.

Row 3 involves pattern development and a choice of harness combinations. For design areas to be woven in plain weave, lift harnesses 1&3. When areas are to be woven in lace, change the treadling and lift harnesses 1,2&3. The treadling is alternated between these two harness combinations as many times as necessary while the shuttle travels selvedge-to-selvedge.

Design Edges in Freeform Design Techniques

When developing a design in any of the freeform design techniques, it is possible to inadvertently leave a warp end raised for several rows where the treadling changes within a row. While the design lines may correspond to those of the cartoon, it is necessary to change the point at which the shuttle enters a new shed by one or two warp ends to accommodate those at the design edge. Observing the point at which the treadling changes for the design should prevent any problem. However, if an exposed warp end does go unobserved, it can be concealed with extra pattern weft yarn once the piece is off the loom.

Knitting and Weaving Combined in Garments

The addition of a knitted cuff or crocheted edge can greatly enhance a garment, and contribute the finishing touch. The vest shown on page 74 is made from two woven strips which are attached at the back and side seams. The knitted waistband adds shape to the vest and provides an attractive finish.

If a knitted edge is to be added, the yarns used for the garment and edge must be compatible. Yarns with no stretch will result in a knitted edge which does not hold its

Knitted waistband added to a woven vest.

Weave Row 4 selvedge-to-selvedge lifting harnesses 2&4.

Row 5 again involves the same choice of harness combinations as Row 3. Areas woven in plain weave lift harnesses 1&3. To weave lace areas, the treadling is changed to lift harnesses 1,2&3. The areas woven in lace in Row 3 are repeated in Row 5. Design areas are changed in Row 3.

Weave Row 6 selvedge-to-selvedge lifting harnesses 2&4.

For areas of a piece in which no treadling changes are involved, either lace or plain weave is woven selvedge-to-selvedge. If lace is woven selvedge-to-selvedge, it is advisable to change the shed before beating, and then place, rather than beat, the row into position. This prevents the lace from compacting too much.

When developing a design in freeform bronson lace, it is wise to change a design line by a complete double float (one entire threading and treadling sequence). However, it is also possible to change a design line by one-half of a threading unit, one warp float.

Freeform bronson lace involves just warp floats on the fabric surface. Therefore, only warp floats are considered when changing the design by one float. It is best to involve a single warp float only in the development of a vertical design line. Changing the horizontal design line using the warp floats necessitates weaving one-half of the warp float length. This resembles an error rather than an intended treadling. The use of one warp float to change a design line is included in the draw-down of *Figure 8-3A*.

Weft Inlay

The addition of weft inlay yarns is very attractive when used with freeform bronson lace. Weft inlay may be added in either one or three rows of the six-row treadling sequence. *Figure 8-4* gives the Table of Harness Combinations and Treadling for the addition of weft inlay yarns in three rows.

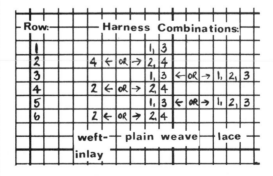

Fig. 8-4. Freeform bronson lace and weft inlay. Table of Harness Combinations and Treadling.

Notice in *Figure 8-4* that inlay weft yarns are added in rows other than those involving pattern development. Weft inlay results in weft floats over plain weave, and a distinct weave structure which is not that of the pattern rows.

When weaving rows which involve the addition of weft inlay, first throw the ground shuttle selvedge-to-selvedge lifting harnesses 2&4. Change the treadling using the appropriate weft-faced harness combination, and add the inlay yarns from the underside of the piece as described in Chapter 2. *Photo 8-3* is an enlargement of the area in which weft inlay has been added to three rows of the six-row treadling sequence.

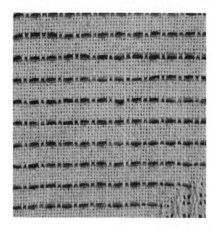

Ph. 8-4. Enlargement of an area in which weft inlay has been added in one row out of six.

Ph. 8-3. Enlargement of an area in which weft inlay has been added in three rows out of six.

If the weft inlay yarn is added only in Row 2, instead of Rows 2,4 and 6, it is possible to create a subtle color effect. An enlargement of the area of a piece in which this method has been used is shown in *Photo 8-4*.

Suitable Projects

Freeform bronson lace, as lace huck, results in a soft material with excellent drape. Projects suitable for freeform bronson lace include table linens, fine hand towels, yardage, blankets, pillows, accessories, and wallhangings. Refer to Appendix A for details.

shape. This may be the desired effect, or it may not. While the yarn used for the knitted edge need not be one used in the fabric, the garment and finishing appear more compatible if the same yarn is used.

To add a knitted cuff, neckline, or waistband, it is necessary first to machine-stitch the edge to which the knitting will be added. A zig-zag stitch works very well. Turn the edge under 1/4" after it is stitched, and pick up the stitches for knitting just above the turned and stitched edge. The stitches picked up for knitting will cover the turned edge, concealing it. Care must be taken to gauge the number of stitches for the knitted edge to prevent the edge from being too loose or tight. It is a good idea to knit a gauge prior to picking up 'he stitches, and figure the total number of stitches needed.

"In an imperfect work, time is an ingredient; but into a perfect work, time does not enter."
Henry David Thoreau

Ph. 8-5. Tablerunner woven in 5/2 Verel. The design motif and colors are derived from the wallpaper shown in the background. Woven by the author.

Ph. 8-6. Tablerunner in 5/2 Verel. Woven by Mimi Pope.

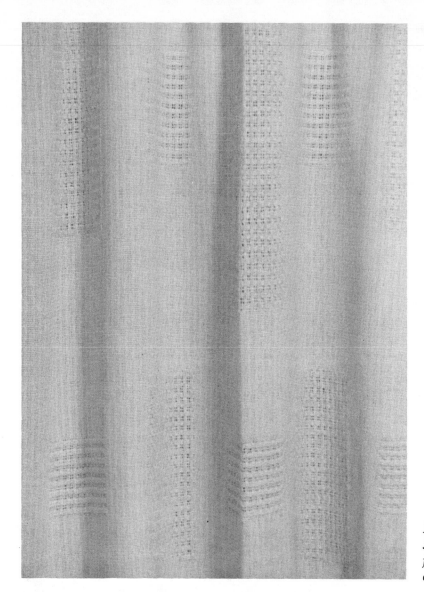

Ph. 8-7. Curtains woven with two colors of 5/2 Verel. One half of the blocks involve warp floats of one color; the other half, weft floats of the second color. Woven by Deb Macke.

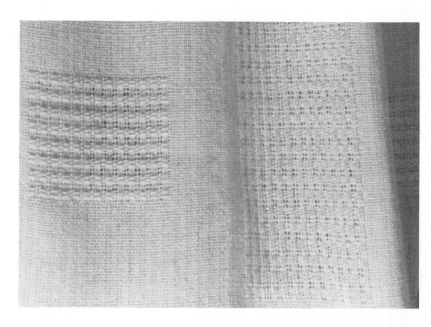

Ph. 8-8. Enlargement of an area of the curtains in Ph. 8-7.

Ph. 8-9. Framed wallhanging of a dunes scene, woven in 5/2 Verel with weft inlay. Woven by Mimi Pope.

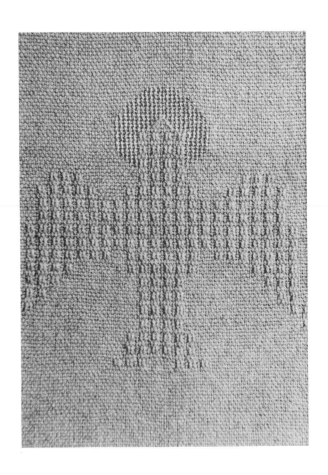

(Above)
Ph. 8-10. Enlargement of an area of the dunes scene in Ph. 8-9 to show areas of weft inlay.

(Left)
Ph. 8-11. Dove woven in 5/2 Verel with weft inlay of gold. Woven by Mimi Pope.

9.

Brocade

The Brocade Technique

Brocade qualifies only marginally as a freeform design technique. However, two-dimensional freeform designs can be woven in brocade and, therefore, the weaver is afforded an additional versatile technique.

Brocade involves a plain weave fabric over which weft-faced twill is woven in pattern. Because these weaves can be woven using the same four-harness threading (harnesses 1,2,3,4), they are often used alternately in a fabric, or are combined as they are in brocade *(Photo 9-1)*.

Ph. 9-1. Detail of piece woven in brocade with straight weft-faced twill.

among the voyagers who brought these silks to Italy via the so-called "silk routes". During this period, a tremendous amount of raw silk, in addition to fabrics, was brought to Europe. Many houses opened in Italy during the 13th and 14th Centuries for the manufacture of silk fabrics, including elaborately brocaded yardage. The Italian brocaded silks understandably bore resemblance to the Chinese fabrics, both in color and design.

The fabric shown in the following photo was woven in Japan during the Edo Period (1615-1868) for use as an obi (sash). The design is one which might well have been used several centuries prior to that time in China, Japan, or Italy. The floral pattern is elaborate and the thread used for brocade is gold wrapped around a linen core.

18th Century Japanese brocaded fabric.

"I am a part of all that I have met;
Yet all experience is an arch
wherethro'
Gleams that untravell'd world,
whose margin fades
For ever and for ever when I move."
Tennyson - *Ulysses*

To weave brocade, a moderately fine warp is sett to square and is threaded on harnesses 1,2,3,4 selvedge-to-selvedge. The warp is usually of cotton, wool with little stretch, or a strong synthetic yarn. Linen may also be used for brocade, and is the only freeform design technique for which it is an appropriate warp yarn. Two weft yarns are needed; a ground yarn the size and color of the warp, and a pattern weft twice the size of the ground and in a contrasting color.

The weaving of brocade is quite different from other freeform design techniques as illustrated in the Table of Harness Combinations and Treadling *(Figure 9-1)*.

Row:	Harness Combinations:
1	1, 3
2	1
3	2, 4
4	2
5	1, 3
6	3
7	2, 4
8	4

Fig. 9-1. Brocade with straight weft-faced twill: Table of Harness Combinations and Treadling.

It would appear from the Table in *Figure 9-1* that no treadling changes occur within the pattern rows, and that is correct. All of the odd-numbered rows in the Table are ground rows. They are woven using the ground weft, and involve no pattern development. The shuttle for these rows is thrown selvedge-to-selvedge alternately lifting harnesses 1&3, and 2&4. The even-numbered rows are the pattern rows which use the pattern weft. The treadling sequence for the pattern rows is that of a weft-faced straight twill, lifting harnesses 1,2,3&4.

Row 1 is woven with the ground weft, which is thrown selvedge-to-selvedge lifting harnesses 1&3. The pattern row which follows lifts harnesses which allow the pattern weft to cover the ground weft. This means that one or the other of the harnesses involved in the preceding ground row remains raised, either harness 1 or 3. Harness 1 remains raised for the first pattern row (Row 2).

The pattern weft yarn is woven through this shed, traveling as far as the design dictates. At the point in the row where the design changes, the maneuvering of the pattern weft differs from other freeform design techniques. Instead of a treadling change from one weave structure to another as with other freeform design techniques, the pattern weft in brocade simply drops under the entire warp wherever it is not to show on the fabric surface. It enters the shed again when the design dictates. This certainly is one of the easier methods of developing a design area!

Again referring to the above Table in *Figure 9-1*, Row 3 is a ground row lifting harnesses 2&4. Follow with a pattern weft row (Row 4), in which harness 2 remains lifted. Again, the pattern weft yarn travels through the shed, dropping beneath the warp wherever it is not to show on the fabric surface. Rows 5 through 8 are woven in the same fashion, with a ground row woven, to be followed by a pattern weft row which lifts one of the harnesses of the preceding row.

It is also possible to weave brocade with a weft-faced broken twill treadling sequence. The procedure is the same as brocade woven with straight twill treadling (*Figure 9-2* and *Photo 9-2*).

Brocade with broken weft-faced twill.

Ph. 9-2. Enlargement of one area of a sampler.

Fig. 9-2. Table of Harness Combinations and Treadling.

Row:	Harness Combinations:		
1		1, 3	
2		1	
3		2, 4	
4		3	
5		1, 3	
6		2	
7		2, 4	
8		4	

Notice with broken twill, that the treadling for pattern rows in Rows 4 and 6 does not involve either harness of the preceding ground row. The pattern weft will, therefore, not cover the ground as completely as in straight twill. The broken twill treadling is included because it is effective in the development of design motifs involving curved lines.

There may be areas of a piece which require no treadling changes. If the pattern weft is to show on the fabric surface, it is woven following each ground weft, treadling the appropriate harness combinations. If the pattern weft is not to show, the ground rows are woven in the usual manner and the pattern weft is eliminated.

There is one difficulty with brocade which deserves attention. When the pattern weft drops under the warp to be carried on the back of the weaving, there is a tendency for the carried pattern weft to pull and distort the fabric. Pattern weft yarns with any amount of stretch should be avoided for this reason, as well as those yarns which will shrink more than the warp and ground weft when washed or ironed. Brocade, as might be imagined, is not a reversible weave!

Ph. 9-3. Reverse side of the brocade sampler woven in broken twill.

Paisley

The famous paisley shawls were woven, first in a tapestry technique, and later using the brocade technique. The method of brocade was quicker than tapestry and eliminated the small bumps in the fabric which occured wherever two weft yarns came together and interlocked.

When brocade was first used for the weaving of paisley shawls, the many pattern weft yarns were carried on the back from one design area to another. Later, these carried wefts were clipped, giving the back of the shawl a velvety appearance. Because the ground weave was firm, there was no danger of the brocade wefts coming out.

The shawl in the accompanying Photos was woven in the early to middle 1800s using the brocade technique. The ground was plain weave and each brocade row was added in the same plain weave shed as the preceding ground row. Because the warp was very fine and the sett not too close, it was possible for the brocade weft to cover the ground and provide a solid design area.

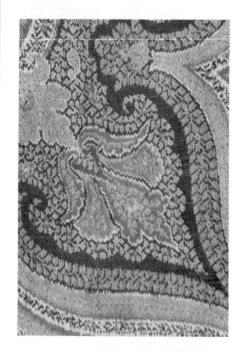

Enlargement of an area of a 19th century paisley shawl.

92

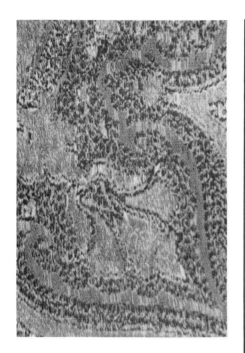

Reverse side of the shawl.

Ph. 9-4. Enlargement of one area of a tablerunner in which weft inlay yarns have been used.

Weft Inlay

Weft inlay yarns can easily be added to brocade. The pattern weft drops to the underside of the weaving where weft inlay yarns are to be added. Then, using the same pattern weft treadling, the weft inlay yarns are added from the underside of the piece, as described in Chapter 2. *Photo 9-4* is an enlargement of an area of a table-runner in which weft inlay yarns have been added.

Suitable Projects

Brocade results in a medium to medium-heavy fabric which has only fair drape because of the pattern weft yarns carried on the back of the piece. Projects woven in brocade should be backed to protect the carried pattern weft yarns. Suitable projects for brocade include heavier outer wear, accessories, pillows, upholstery, border embellishment on plain weave pieces, and bedspreads (if the pattern weft yarns are carried only a short distance). Refer to Appendix A for details.

(Left)
Ph. 9-5. Tablerunner of 5/2 cotton and medium weight wool in straight twill brocade. Woven by the author.

(Below)
Ph. 9-6. Sampler with broken twill brocade. Woven by Lois Crocker.

Ph. 9-7. Wallhanging entitled "Renaissance Man" of 10/2 linen and fine weight wool, woven in broken twill brocade with areas of weft inlay. Woven by the author.

Section II

Section II involves techniques based on weaves presented in Section I. These weaves result in fabrics which are heavier than those of the freeform techniques, ranging from medium to heavy weight. A number of the weaves are reversible. The threading and the pairs of harness combinations for each double weft technique are the same as those of Section I. Two pattern weft yarns, *A* and *B*, are used, resulting in fabrics which are totally weft-faced on both sides.

The double weft techniques involve three basic types. The lighter weight techniques are presented first. These weaves are sett to square as are the freeform techniques. Because the warp is sett closely, the weft is prevented from compacting, which allows the warp to show as part of the design. Included are double weft twill, double weft Summer & Winter, and double weft Marsh.

The next two techniques are broadweft Summer & Winter, and broadweft Ms & Os. These weaves result in considerably heavier fabrics. They are woven like double weft techniques, but the warp is sleyed with fewer ends per inch, and the weft compacts with no warp visible. Broad weft Summer & Winter is better known as "shaft-switching".

Freeform Finnweave and freeform double weave (more familiar as "double weave pick-up") constitute the final pair of techniques. For these techniques, the warp is divided into two separate layers which are interchanged at certain points for pattern development. While the results of both freeform double weave and Finnweave are identical to traditional fabrics woven using the same techniques, weaving them as freeform design techniques greatly simplifies the weaving procedure of both.

10.

Double Weft Twill

Introduction

Double weft twill looks similar to freeform twill. The weight of warp and weft yarns and the sett of the warp are the same. However, double weft twill involves the use of two pattern weft yarns instead of one. The fabric created is weft-faced on both sides, and is heavier than fabric woven in freeform twill.

The threading for double weft twill is the same as freeform twill, harnesses 1,2,3,4, repeated selvedge-to-selvedge. The pairs of harness combinations for each row are also the same: harness combination 1 or 1,2&3; 2 or 1,2&4; 3 or 1,3&4; 4 or 2,3&4. A medium to fine warp yarn is used (comparable to 5/2 cotton or finer). The warp is sett to square, which means weaving as many rows per inch as there are warp ends per inch. If 5/2 cotton is the warp, the sett to square is 15 ends per inch.

Two pattern weft yarns are required for double weft twill. Each should be close to the size of the warp, and in colors which contrast one another as well as the warp. Each pattern weft yarn should be approximately twice the size of the warp and the same size as one another.

Straight Double Weft Twill

The Table of Harness Combinations and Treadling for straight double weft twill is given in *Figure 10-1*. A Photo of straight double weft twill is shown in *Photo 10-1*.

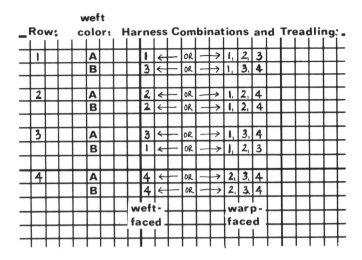

Row	weft color	Harness Combinations and Treadling				
1	A	1	←	OR	→	1, 2, 3
	B	3	←	OR	→	1, 3, 4
2	A	2	←	OR	→	1, 2, 4
	B	2	←	OR	→	1, 2, 4
3	A	3	←	OR	→	1, 3, 4
	B	1	←	OR	→	1, 2, 3
4	A	4	←	OR	→	2, 3, 4
	B	4	←	OR	→	2, 3, 4
		weft-faced			warp-faced	

Fig. 10-1. Straight freeform twill: Table of Harness Combinations and Treadling.

Ph. 10-1. Enlargement of an area of a piece woven in straight double weft twill.

Preparing Handwoven Fabric For Sewing

Handwoven yardage is no more difficult to handle than commercial fabrics. Once the fabric is off the loom, stitch across both ends to secure the warp ends and weft. Test the warp and weft yarns for color fastness.

Before the fabric can be cut, it must be shrunk and squared. The natural fibers — cotton, wool, linen, and silk — all shrink when washed in hot water. Thoroughly soak fabrics woven in cotton, linen and silk, and put the wet material into warm water. Bring the water to 160 to 180° and allow it to cool to room temperature. The pot should be large enough to allow ample space around the fabric. If the piece is quite large, it may be necessary to use the washing machine. If the washing machine is used, fill it with water 160 to 180°. Wet the fabric thoroughly in tepid water, and then put it into the washing machine. Allow it to sit until the water becomes cool. Set the machine to spin, and spin the water out.

Squeeze and press additional water out of the fabric. Do not wring the fabric since wrinkles, particularly in linen, may become permanent. Lay the fabric out to dry, being careful to square the warp and weft throughout the fabric. When barely damp, iron the fabric. It can now be cut without fear of unraveling.

Wool is handled in much the same way as cotton, linen and silk. However, care must be taken not to immerse wool in very hot or cold water, as this can cause felting. The wool fabric should be thoroughly soaked in cool water and then placed in a suitably large pot filled with tepid water. Bring the water slowly to 160°. Let the water cool to room temperature without removing the fabric. Squeeze the water from the fabric and lay it out to dry.

Notice in *Figure 10-1* that both pattern weft yarns, *A* and *B*, are woven in each row. Different pairs of harness combinations are treadled for each pattern weft yarn in Rows 1 & 3, and the same pair of harness combinations is treadled for both pattern weft yarns in Rows 2 & 4. This particular treadling sequence for each of the pattern weft yarns is necessary if the twill diagonals of the two design areas are to oppose one another.

All techniques in Section II are woven in the same manner. Therefore, an understanding of the treadling procedure for double weft twill facilitates the weaving of the other techniques.

The treadling sequence for double weft twill follows, using the design motif in *Photo 10-1*. Pattern weft *A* is the dark color in *Photo 10-1*, and pattern weft *B* is the light color.

Every row begins with pattern weft *A* and is followed by pattern weft *B*. It is easy to keep track of the shuttles if they both start at the same selvedge for each row. Following the design motif in *Photo*

10-1, Row 1 begins with pattern weft A and both shuttles are at the left selvedge. Since pattern weft A is woven on the fabric surface at the left selvedge, lift harness 1 (weft-faced). Weave with pattern weft A as far through the shed as the design dictates. At the point where pattern weft A is to be woven on the underside of the fabric, (no longer appearing on the fabric surface), change the treadling to lift harnesses 1,2&3 (warp-faced), and continue through the shed to the point at which the treadling changes. At the point where pattern weft A is again woven on the fabric surface, lift harness 1 (weft-faced). The design in *Photo 10-1* involves only two changes in treadling, and pattern weft A is therefore carried to the right selvedge.

Begin pattern weft B at the left selvedge. Because pattern weft A is woven on the fabric surface at the left selvedge (weft-faced), pattern weft B must be treadled to do the opposite and appear on the underside of the fabric (warp-faced). The first treadling for pattern weft B therefore is harness combination 1,3&4. The shuttle travels in this shed to the point at which pattern weft A changes treadling to appear on the underside of the fabric (warp-faced). Pattern weft B must also change treadling to appear on the fabric surface (weft-faced). Lift harness 3. Take the shuttle in this shed to the point where the treadling again changes. Where pattern weft A is woven on the fabric surface (weft-faced), change the treadling and lift harnesses 1,3&4 for pattern weft B (warp-faced). Pattern weft B appears on the underside of the fabric. Since this is the final treadling change, the shuttle travels to the right selvedge.

The design is developed when weaving with pattern weft A, and the treadling is changed from one harness combination to the other as many times as the design dictates within that row. Pattern weft B completes the design established with pattern weft A. A side view of the passage of pattern wefts A and B for each of the four rows of straight double weft twill is given in *Figure 10-2*.

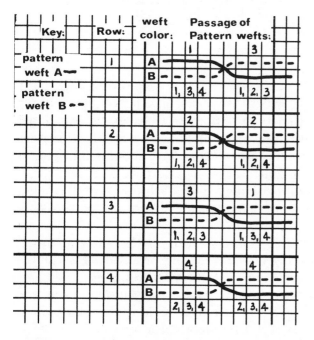

Fig. 10-2. Side view of the passage of pattern wefts A and B in the four rows of straight double weft twill.

Row 2 of *Figure 10-1* involves the same pair of harness combinations for pattern wefts A and B, harness 2 for weft-faced areas and harnesses 1,2&4 for warp-faced areas. Both shuttles are now at

Synthetic yarns may or may not shrink. If the fabric is woven of material which does not shrink, steam press it under a towel, being careful to follow any instructions for care of that yarn. Steam pressing crimps the warp and weft yarns, and assures that they will hold their position when cut.

Fulling Wool Fabric

Wool fabric can be made very soft by a special fulling method. The fulling may be done in addition to shrinking the fabric in preparation for sewing. Fill the washing machine with tepid water. Add 1/2 cup protein hair rinse. Set the machine to agitate the water for one minute. Add wet wool fabric. Agitate on a gentle cycle for 30 seconds. Leave the fabric in the water 15 additional minutes. Spin dry. Roll the fabric in towels to remove the excess water, and lay it out flat to dry.

Use the Selvedge in Sewing

When laying out a pattern on handwoven fabric, use selvedges wherever possible. This avoids raveling and provides a firm seam.

"I expect to pass through this world but once. Any good thing, therefore, that I can do, or any kindness I can show to any fellow human being, let me do it now. Let me not defer nor neglect it; for I shall not pass this way again."
Stephen Grellet

Cutting Handwoven Fabric

Fabric which is handwoven may have somewhat greater give than commercial fabrics, and often is more loosely woven. Take considerable care positioning the fabric and placing and pinning the pattern. If the fabric is loosely woven, it may be necessary to use a fabric glue on curved edges as the pattern is cut to help hold the yarns in place. It is also a good idea to stabilize these curves using a loose stitch. It is not necessary to stitch all cut edges unless the fabric ravels excessively.

Hem Your Placemats!

There is no yarn available which will not ravel or shred when put repeatedly through the washer and dryer. Therefore, fringed placemats which are washed frequently will need to be hemmed at some point in time. Hemming placemats which previously have been fringed may result in mats the size of hot pads. Avoid the problem altogether by weaving an extra 1 1/2" per mat (3/4" per hem) and hemming your placemats. Do the job right the first time!

the right selvedge. Starting with pattern weft *A*, lift harness 2 (weft-faced), since pattern weft *A* appears on the fabric surface at the right selvedge. Take the shuttle through the shed to the point where the treadling changes. Where pattern weft *A* is woven on the underside of the fabric (warp-faced), change the treadling and lift harnesses 1,2&4. The shuttle travels in this shed to the next treadling change. At the point where pattern weft *A* is again woven on the fabric surface, lift harness 2 (weft-faced) and take the shuttle to the left selvedge.

Pattern weft *B* follows, also from the right selvedge. Because pattern weft *B* is woven on the underside of the fabric at the right selvedge, lift harnesses 1,2&4 (warp-faced). In the center of the design, where pattern weft *A* changes to warp-faced treadling, lift harness 2 for pattern weft *B* (weft-faced). Take the shuttle through this shed to the next treadling change. Where pattern weft *A* changes to weft-faced treadling, lift harnesses 1,2&4 for pattern weft *B* (warp-faced). The shuttle travels to the left selvedge.

Row 3 of *Figure 10-1* again involves a different pair of harness combinations for pattern wefts *A* and *B*. Starting with pattern weft *A* at the left selvedge, lift harness 3, since pattern weft *A* is woven on the fabric surface at the left selvedge. At the point where pattern weft *A* changes treadling and appears on the underside of the fabric, lift harnesses 1,3&4 (warp-faced). Where pattern weft *A* is again woven on the fabric surface, change the treadling and lift harness 3 (weft-faced). The shuttle travels to the right selvedge.

Pattern weft B of Row 3 also starts at the left selvedge. Lift harnesses 1,2&3 (warp-faced), since pattern weft *B* appears on the underside of the fabric at the left selvedge. Where pattern weft *A* changes to warp-faced treadling, change treadling and lift harness 1 for pattern weft *B* (weft-faced). At the next point where the treadling changes and pattern weft *A* is woven on the fabric surface (weft-faced), pattern weft *B* is woven on the underside of the fabric. Lift harnesses 1,2&3 (warp-faced) and take the shuttle to the right selvedge.

Pattern wefts *A* and *B* use the same pair of harness combinations in Row 4, harness 4 for weft-faced areas, and harnesses 2,3&4 for warp-faced areas. Pattern weft *A* starts at the right selvedge. Lift harness 4 (weft-faced), as pattern weft *A* is woven on the fabric surface at the right selvedge. Where the treadling changes and pattern weft *A* is woven on the underside of the fabric, lift harnesses 2,3&4 (warp-faced). At the point where pattern weft *A* is again woven on the fabric surface, lift harness 4. The shuttle travels to the left selvedge.

Pattern weft *B* of Row 4 follows, also from the right selvedge. Pattern weft *B* is woven on the underside of the fabric at the right selvedge, and therefore lifts harnesses 2,3&4 (warp-faced). Where the treadling changes to warp-faced for pattern weft *A*, lift harness 4 for pattern weft *B* (weft-faced), weaving pattern weft *B* on the fabric surface. Take the shuttle to the point where pattern weft *A* is again woven on the fabric surface (weft-faced). Change the treadling and lift harnesses 2,3&4 for pattern weft *B*. The shuttle continues in this warp-faced shed to the left selvedge. Repeat these four rows for areas of the piece which involve treadling changes within each row. Notice that the design in *Photo 10-1* requires two treadling changes in each row for part of the design motif, and four treadling changes

101

in each row in the center part of the design.

For areas of the piece which require no treadling changes within the rows, the treadling sequence is somewhat different. For the pattern weft yarn which is to be woven on the fabric surface, treadle the appropriate weft-faced harness combination, and throw the shuttle selvedge-to-selvedge. Follow each weft-faced shot with the appropriate warp-faced treadling, throwing the second pattern weft shuttle selvedge-to-selvedge. This second pattern weft yarn appears on the underside of the fabric. It is necessary to throw both shuttles for each row in order to retain the weave structure, even though only one is woven on the fabric surface.

Broken Double Weft Twill

Broken double weft twill is woven in the same manner as straight double weft twill. Because there are no opposing diagonal lines involved in broken twill, it is possible to use the same pair of harness combinations for both pattern weft yarns in each row. Broken double weft twill is useful when weaving designs which include curved lines. The Table of Harness Combinations and Treadling (*Figure 10-3A*), and diagram of the passage of pattern wefts (*10-3B*) are given. A close-up of the technique appears in *Photo 10-2*.

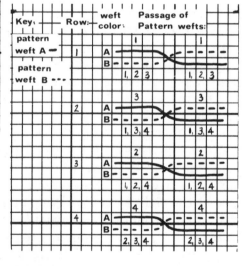

Broken double weft twill.

Fig. 10-3A. Table of Harness Combinations and Treadling.

Fig. 10-3B. Side view of the passage of pattern weft yarns in the four rows.

Ph. 10-2. Enlargement of the area of a piece woven in broken double weft twill.

"Bless, O Chief of generous chiefs,
My loom and everything a-near me,
Bless me in my every action,
Make Thou me safe while I live."
Loom Blessing (Outer Isles)

Mounting Wallhangings

Weaving a wallhanging is one thing; hanging it properly is quite another! The most commonly used method for hanging a piece is to fold the top to the back and stitch it down. A rod is placed through the opening at the top of the hanging, and the piece is then supported by the rod. This is fine for many hangings, particularly those which are light weight.

The problem occurs when hanging a heavy piece, or one which is fragile either because of age or choice of yarns and/or technique. For these pieces, it is best to use a different method of hanging which removes the stress from the warp and distributes stress more evenly throughout the fabric.

Finish the top of the wallhanging by turning the top edge back, tucking the warp ends under. Handstitch the edge down. Cut a piece of muslin the width of the wallhanging and 3-4" long. Turn the edges of the muslin under on all four sides and machine stitch to provide a finished edge. On the right side of the muslin, center and sew a Velcro® strip the length of the muslin (the width of the wallhanging). Handstitch the muslin and Velcro® across the back of the wallhanging 1-2" from the top. The top of the muslin should be on the turned edge of the wallhanging, the bottom on the body of the piece. Handstitch all four sides of the muslin to the wallhanging.

The second half of the Velcro® strip is affixed to the wall, either directly or to a mounting which is then hung. The wallhanging is then hung by pressing the two halves of the Velcro® strips together.

If the wallhanging is heavy, it may be necessary to add a second muslin strip with Velcro® 2/3 of the distance from the top of the hanging. It is also possible to add a rod through the top of the wallhanging in the conventional manner and support the hanging by the rod as well as the Velcro® strips.

In Row 1, pattern weft A is woven first. In areas of the design in which pattern weft A is woven on the fabric surface (weft-faced), lift harness 1. In areas of the design in which pattern weft A appears on the underside of the fabric (warp-faced), change the treadling and lift harnesses 1,2&3 (warp-faced). These harness combinations are alternated from one to the other as many times as the design dictates.

Begin the pattern weft B shuttle at the same selvedge as pattern weft A, using the same pair of harness combinations but in positions opposite pattern weft A. Wherever pattern weft A is woven weft-faced, lift harnesses 1,2&3 for pattern weft B (warp-faced). Where pattern weft A is woven warp-faced, lift harness 1 for pattern weft B (weft-faced).

For Row 2, pattern weft A is woven first. Lift harness 3 in areas in which pattern weft A is woven on the fabric surface (weft-faced). Change the treadling and lift harnesses 1,3&4 in areas in which it appears on the underside of the fabric (warp-faced). Pattern weft B follows. Where pattern weft A is woven weft-faced, lift harnesses 1,3&4 for pattern weft B (warp-faced). Where pattern weft A is woven warp-faced, lift harness 3 for pattern weft B (weft-faced).

In Row 3, using pattern weft A, lift harness 2 for weft-faced areas woven on the fabric surface. Change the treadling and lift harnesses 1,2&4 in areas where pattern weft A appears on the underside of the fabric (warp-faced). Pattern weft B follows, using the same pair of harness combinations, but in positions opposite pattern weft A. Where pattern weft A is woven warp-faced, lift harness 2 for pattern weft B (weft-faced). Where pattern weft A is woven weft-faced, lift harnesses 1,2&4 for pattern weft B (warp-faced).

Row 4 involves harness 4 for weft-faced areas and harnesses 2,3&4 for warp-faced areas. Pattern weft A is again woven first. Lift harness 4 in areas where pattern weft A is woven on the fabric surface (weft-faced). Change the treadling and lift harnesses 2,3&4 where it appears on the underside of the fabric (warp-faced). Pattern weft B follows using the same harness combinations but in positions opposite pattern weft A. Where pattern weft A is woven warp-faced, lift harness 4 for pattern weft B (weft-faced). Where pattern weft A is woven weft-faced, lift harnesses 2,3&4 for pattern weft B (warp-faced). This four-row sequence is repeated for areas of a piece in which treadling changes occur within the rows.

In areas requiring no treadling changes, treadle the appropriate weft-faced harness combination for the pattern weft yarn which is to be woven on the fabric surface, and throw that shuttle selvedge-to-selvedge. Follow each weft-faced row with the appropriate warp-faced treadling, throwing the second pattern weft shuttle selvedge-to-selvedge. This second pattern weft yarn appears on the underside of the fabric. As with straight double weft twill, it is necessary to throw both shuttles in each row in order to retain the weave structure, even though only one is woven on the fabric surface.

Combined Double Weft Twill

Just as with freeform twill, it is possible to weave one pattern weft area in a broken treadling sequence, while simultaneously weaving the other area using a straight treadling sequence. The combined treadling is helpful when a distinct difference is desired between the design area and the background. The Table of Harness Combinations and Treadling (*Figure 10-4A*), and diagram of the passage of the pattern wefts (*Figure 10-4B*) are given. An enlargement of an area of a piece woven with straight treadling for the background and broken treadling for the design motif appears in *Photo 10-3*.

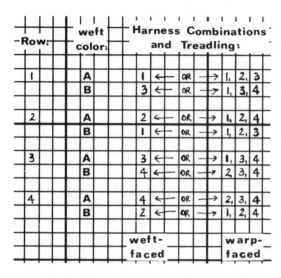

Combined double weft twill.

Fig. 10-4A. Table of Harness Combinations and Treadling. Color A develops the straight twill; color B, the broken twill (left).

Fig. 10-4B. Side view of the passage of pattern weft yarns in the four rows (below).

Ph. 10-3. Enlargement of an area of a piece woven in combined double weft twill.

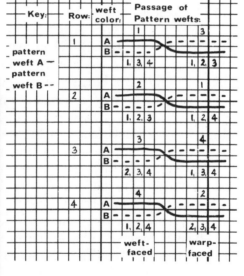

All four rows of *Figure 10-4A* involve different pairs of harness combinations for pattern wefts *A* and *B*. However, the method of weaving is the same as for straight or broken double weft twill.

In Row 1, using pattern weft *A*, lift harness 1 for weft-faced areas which are woven on the fabric surface. For areas which appear on the underside of the fabric, change the treadling and lift harnesses 1,2&3 (warp-faced). These treadlings can be alternated from one to the other as many times as the design dictates. Pattern weft *B* follows. In areas where pattern weft *A* is woven weft-faced, lift harnesses 1,3&4 for pattern weft *B* (warp-faced). In areas where

Ms & Os as Double Weft Technique

It is possible to weave freeform Ms & Os as a double weft technique. It is similar to double weft Summer & Winter in Chapter 11, in fabric weight and drape, and is a slightly more stable weave. Weft inlay yarns are added in the same manner and the projects suitable for double weft Summer & Winter are also suitable for double weft Ms & Os. Because double weft Ms & Os does provide an additional technique with interesting features, it is presented in INSIGHTS.

For Ms & Os woven as a double weft technique, the threading is harnesses 1,2,1,2,3,4,3,4. Sett a 5/2 cotton warp (or comparable) to square. Two pattern weft yarns are necessary which contrast one another and the warp in color. A ground weft is also used which is the color and weight of the warp. The harness combinations used are the same as freeform Ms & Os woven with two pattern wefts (Chapter 5). The Table of Harness Combinations and Treadling for double weft Ms & Os and a diagram of the passage of pattern wefts are given.

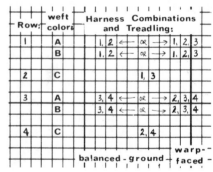

Double weft Ms & Os—Table of Harness Combinations. "Balanced" = "weft-faced".

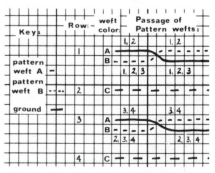

Side view of the passage of pattern and ground weft yarns.

For Row 1, using pattern weft A, lift harnesses 1&2 for areas of the design which are woven on the fabric surface (balanced). Change the treadling and lift harnesses 1,2&3 in areas where pattern weft A appears on the underside of the fabric (warp-faced). Pattern weft B follows using the same harness combinations but in the opposite position to pattern weft A. Where pattern weft A is woven on the fabric surface (balanced), lift harnesses 1,2&3 for pattern weft B (warp-faced). Where pattern weft A is woven warp-faced, lift harnesses 1&2 for pattern weft B (balanced). Row 2 is a ground row thrown selvedge-to-selvedge lifting harnesses 1&3 and using the ground weft (C).

Row 3 is woven exactly like Row 1, but lifting harnesses 3&4 for areas woven on the fabric surface (balanced), and harnesses 2,3&4 for areas which appear on the underside of the fabric (warp-faced). Row 4 is a ground row thrown selvedge-to-selvedge lifting harnesses 2&4 and using the ground weft (C).

A close-up of a sampler is shown as well as a piece woven in double weft Ms & Os.

A close-up of a sampler woven in double weft Ms & Os.

A wallhanging woven in double weft Ms & Os with weft inlay yarns.

pattern weft A is woven warp-faced, lift harness 3 for pattern weft B (weft-faced).

Row 2 is woven in the same manner as Row 1. Begin with pattern weft A. Lift harness 2 in weft-faced area where pattern weft A is woven on the fabric surface, and harnesses 1,2&4 in warp-faced areas where it appears on the underside of the fabric. Pattern weft B follows. In areas where pattern weft A is woven weft-faced, lift harnesses 1,2&3 for pattern weft B (warp-faced). In areas where pattern weft A is woven warp-faced, lift harness 1 for pattern weft B (weft-faced).

In Row 3 using pattern weft A, lift harness 3 in weft-faced areas where it is woven on the fabric surface. Change the treadling and lift harnesses 1,3&4 in warp-faced areas where it appears on the underside of the fabric. Pattern weft B follows. In areas where pattern weft A is woven warp-faced, lift harness 4 for pattern weft B (weft-faced). In areas where pattern weft A is woven weft-faced, lift harnesses 2,3&4 for pattern weft B (warp-faced).

In Row 4 with pattern weft A, lift harness 4 in weft-faced areas where it is woven on the fabric surface, and harnesses 2,3&4 in warp-faced areas where it appears on the underside of the fabric. Pattern weft B follows. In areas where pattern weft A is woven warp-faced, lift harness 2 for pattern weft B (weft-faced). In areas where pattern weft A is woven weft-faced, lift harnesses 1,2&4 for pattern weft B (warp-faced). Repeat this four-row sequence for areas of a piece which involve treadling changes within a row.

For areas of the piece which require no treadling changes within the row, treadle the weft-faced harness combination for the pattern weft yarn which is to be woven on the fabric surface, and throw that shuttle selvedge-to-selvedge. Follow each weft-faced row with the appropriate warp-faced treadling, throwing the second pattern weft shuttle selvedge-to-selvedge. This second pattern weft yarn appears on the underside of the fabric. It is necessary to throw both shuttles in each row in order to retain the weave structure.

Weft Inlay

The use of weft inlay yarns works well only with broken double weft twill. Because the same pair of harness combinations is used for both pattern weft yarns in broken double weft twill, the pattern weft yarns are woven in the same warp-faced shed, making it possible for the weft inlay yarns to cover sufficiently.

Both pattern weft yarns are woven before weft inlay yarns are added. Each pattern weft yarn passes through the area in which weft inlay is to be added treadling the appropriate warp-faced harness combination. After the pattern weft rows have been woven, treadle the weft-faced harness combination for that row, and place the weft inlay yarns, entering and exiting the shed from the underside of the piece as described in Chapter 2. Because two pattern weft yarns are woven before the weft inlay yarn is added, it may be necessary to use a yarn for inlay which is slightly heavier than one pattern weft yarn. The use of a textured yarn for weft inlay also helps cover the pattern weft yarns.

Figure 10-5 shows the side view of the passage of the two pattern weft yarns through the weft inlay area, and the addition of a weft inlay yarn.

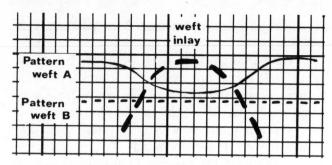

Fig. 10-5. Side view of a row in which weft inlay yarns are added to double weft twill.

Suitable Projects

With the appropriate yarn selection, double weft twill can result in a fabric of medium weight with average to good drape. The weave is best suited for outer wear, accessories, table linens, bedspreads, pillows, upholstery and wallhangings. Refer to Appendix A for details.

(Left)
Ph. 10-4. Vest woven in fine and medium weight wool, using a broken treadling sequence. Woven by Pat Short.

(Right)
Ph. 10-5. Enlargement of one area of the vest shown in Ph. 10-4.

Ph. 10-6. Sampler woven in 5/2 Verel and fine weight wool, in which straight and broken treadling sequences are combined. Woven by the author.

(Left)
Ph. 10-7. Tablerunner woven in 5/2 Verel, in which straight and broken treadling sequences are combined. Woven by Mugs O'Toole.

(Below)
Ph. 10-8. Enlargement of one area of the tablerunner shown in Ph. 10-7.

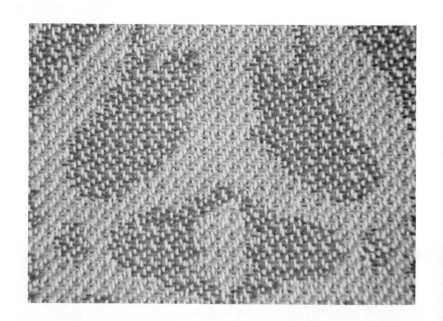

(Left) Ph. 10-9. Sampler in which one half of the piece is woven with a broken treadling sequence; the other half with a straight treadling sequence. (Right) Ph. 10-10. Reverse side of sampler shown in Ph. 10-9, demonstrating the reversibility of the weave. Woven by the author.

11.

Double Weft Summer & Winter

Freeform Technique

Double weft Summer & Winter is threaded the same as freeform Summer & Winter, harnesses 1,2,3,4. The selected warp is sett to square, and a warp comparable to 5/2 cotton (or finer) is the usual choice. If 5/2 cotton is used, the sett to square is 15 ends per inch. The pairs of harness combinations are the same as freeform Summer & Winter and are detailed in *Figure 11-1A*. A diagram of the passage of pattern weft yarns is given in *Figure 11-1B*, and *Photo 11-1* shows a sample woven in double weft Summer & Winter.

Row:	weft color:	Harness Combinations and Treadling				
1	A	1	←	OR	→	1, 2, 4
	B	1	←	OR	→	1, 2, 4
2	A	3	←	OR	→	2, 3, 4
	B	3	←	OR	→	2, 3, 4
		weft-faced			warp-faced	

Double weft Summer & Winter.

Fig. 11-1A. Table of Harness Combinations and Treadling (above).

Fig. 11-1B. Side view of the passage of pattern weft yarns (right).

Key:	Row:	weft color:	Passage of Pattern wefts:				
pattern weft A —	1	A		1			1
		B	—	—	—		—
pattern weft B - - -				1, 2, 4			1, 2, 4
	2	A				3	3
		B	—	—	—		
				2, 3, 4			2, 3, 4

INSIGHTS

A Light Beat When Weaving Double Weft Summer & Winter

The rows of pattern weft in double weft Summer & Winter do not cover the warp completely because of the close sett of the warp. A light touch with the beater when weaving helps assure the lighter weight and drapability of the fabric.

"The life of every man is a seamless garment—its woof his thoughts, its warp his deeds. When for him the roaring loom of Time stops and the thread is broken, foolish people sometimes point to certain spots in the robe and say, 'Oh, why did he not leave that out!' not knowing that every action of man is a sequence from off Fate's spindle."

Elbert Hubbard

Warp Effect With Double Weft Summer & Winter

Harnesses 1 and 3 provide the tie-down on the fabric surface of double weft Summer & Winter. Because the beat is light and the warp is sett to square, these warp ends on harnesses 1 and 3 are evident as part of the weave structure. It is possible to create a subtle shading in a piece by warping with a different color for harnesses 1&3 and 2&4, and then changing the pair of harnesses which appears on the surface of the weave as the piece progresses. The Table of Harness Combinations and Treadling which allows harnesses 2&4 to be woven on the fabric surface is given.

Row:	weft color:	Harness Combinations and Treadling:					
1	A	2	←	OR	→	1, 2, 3
	B	2	←	OR	→	1, 2, 3
2	A	4	←	OR	→	1, 3, 4
	B	4	←	OR	→	1, 3, 4
		weft-faced				warp-faced

Double weft Summer & Winter: Table of Harness Combination and Treadling with harnesses 2&4 on the fabric surface.

A close-up of a piece is shown in which harnesses 1 and 3 are threaded with white warp, and harnesses 2 and 4 are threaded with blue warp. Notice the point at which the harness combinations change, bringing the opposite pair of harnesses to the surface of the fabric.

"Mankind is a weaver, who, from the wrong side, works on the carpet of time. The day will come when we will see the right side and understand the grandeur of the pattern we, with our hands, have woven through the centuries without seeing anything but a tangle of strings."
Lamertine

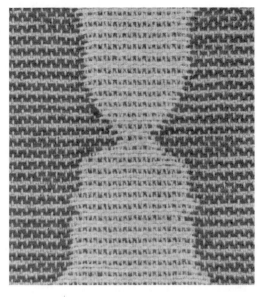

Ph. 11-1. Sample woven in double weft Summer & Winter.

Two pattern weft yarns, *A & B*, are necessary to weave double weft Summer & Winter. Each yarn is twice the size of the warp and in colors which contrast one another. One pattern weft yarn should be close to the color of the warp. No ground weft is used. In *Photo 11-1*, the dark color is designated pattern weft *A*; the light color pattern weft *B*.

Row 1 involves the same pair of harness combinations for both pattern weft yarns: harness 1 (weft-faced), and harnesses 1,2&4 (warp-faced). Begin Row 1 with pattern weft *A*, and place both shuttles at the left selvedge. Following the design motif in *Photo 11-1*, since pattern weft *A* is woven on the fabric surface at the left selvedge, lift harness 1 (weft-faced). Weave with pattern weft *A* as far through the shed as the design dictates. Where pattern weft *A* is to be woven on the underside of the fabric, change the treadling and lift harnesses 1,2&4 (warp-faced), and carry the shuttle through that shed to the point at which the treadling again changes. Where pattern weft *A* is woven on the fabric surface, lift harness 1 (weft-faced). Take the shuttle to the right selvedge.

Pattern weft *B* involves the same pair of harness combinations as pattern weft *A*, but in positions opposite pattern weft *A*. Begin pattern weft *B* at the left selvedge. Because pattern weft *A* is woven on the fabric surface at the left selvedge (weft-faced), lift harnesses 1,2&4 for pattern weft *B* (warp-faced). Where pattern weft *A* changes to warp-faced treadling, lift harness 1 for pattern weft *B* (weft-faced). Take the shuttle through this shed to the next treadling change. Where pattern weft *A* is again woven weft-faced, lift harnesses 1,2&4 for pattern weft *B* (warp-faced). The shuttle travels to the right selvedge.

The same pair of harness combinations is involved for both pattern weft yarns in Row 2: harness 3 (weft-faced), and harnesses 2,3&4 (warp-faced). Beginning Row 2 with pattern weft *A*, lift harness 3 (weft-faced), since pattern weft *A* is woven on the fabric surface at the right selvedge. Where the treadling changes and pattern weft *A* appears on the underside of the fabric, change the treadling and lift harnesses 2,3&4 (warp-faced). At the point where pattern weft *A* is again woven on the fabric surface, change the treadling sand lift harness 3 (weft-faced). The shuttle travels to the left selvedge.

Pattern weft *B* follows, using the same pair of harness combinations as pattern weft *A*, but in opposite positions. Because pattern weft *A* is woven on the fabric surface at the right selvedge (weft-faced), lift harnesses 2,3&4 for pattern weft *B* (warp-faced). Where pattern weft *A* appears on the underside of the fabric (warp-faced), change the treadling and lift harness 3 for pattern weft *B* (weft-faced). At the point where pattern weft *A* is again woven on the fabric surface, lift harnesses 2,3&4 for pattern weft *B* (warp-faced), and take the shuttle to the left selvedge. No ground weft is involved. These two rows are repeated in areas of the fabric which involve treadling changes within each row.

In areas involving no treadling changes, treadle the appropriate weft-faced harness combination for the pattern weft yarn which is to be woven on the fabric surface. Throw that shuttle selvedge-to-selvedge. Follow each weft-faced row with the appropriate warp-faced treadling, throwing the second pattern weft shuttle selvedge-to-selvedge to appear on the underside of the fabric.

Weft Inlay

Both pattern weft yarns of a row are woven before weft inlay yarns are added. Each pattern weft yarn for Rows 1 and 2 passes through the area in which weft inlay is to be added treadling the warp-faced harness combination for that row. After both pattern weft yarns have been woven, treadle the appropriate weft-faced harness combination and add the weft inlay yarns, entering and exiting the shed from the underside of the fabric as described in Chapter 2. *Photo 11-2* shows a piece in which weft inlay yarns have been added.

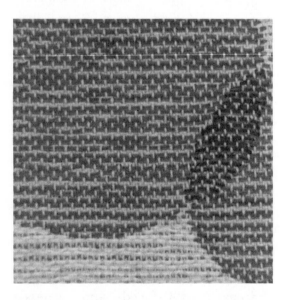

Ph. 11-2. Sample woven in double weft Summer & Winter, to which weft inlay yarns have been added.

Suitable Projects

Double weft Summer & Winter results in a fabric of medium weight with average to good drape. The fabric has quite a bit of give which should be considered when contemplating its use for clothing. The weave is most suitable for projects which will not cause the fabric to stretch. These include vests, accessories, border designs, and table linens. Refer to Appendix A for details.

Matching the Patterns in Handwoven Garments

Consider the size of the design repeat for garments when creating a plaid or check, or a design motif which repeats. It takes considerable experience to weave with exactly the same beat throughout a piece of fabric. Therefore, if the design motif or plaid is large, the repeats may be slightly different sizes. This will cause difficulty when matching two cut pieces for garments. Particularly the less experienced weaver or seamstress should consider a small design motif or plaid which will match up easily.

Loom-shaped Garments Are More Often Mis-shaped

Many weavers hesitate to cut into handwoven fabric, and would rather weave the garment on the loom as it should be shaped on the person. This is seldom a successful approach! The hand of the shaped fabric will change as the shape of the weaving is altered on the loom. Warp may become looser, weft rows more tightly compacted. No shape created on the loom can be tailored on the loom (and usually off) to successfully meet the idiosyncrasies of the human form!

"The purpose of life is not to be happy. The purpose of life is to *matter*, to be productive, to have it make some difference that you lived at all. Happiness, in the ancient, noble sense, means self-fulfillment —and is given to those who use to the fullest whatever talents God or luck or fate bestowed upon them. Happiness, to me, lies in stretching to the farthest boundaries of which we are capable, the resources of the mind and heart."
Leo Rosten

(Right)
Ph 11-3. Wallhanging entitled "Plum Branch" woven in 10/2 linen and handspun and dyed wool, with areas of weft inlay. Woven by the author.

(Below)
Ph. 11-4. Enlargement of one area of "Plum Branch".

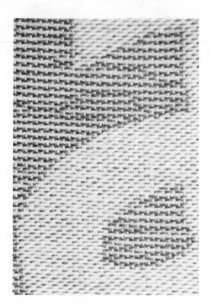

12.

Double Weft Marsh

Freeform Technique

Double weft Marsh is a variation of double weft Summer & Winter. The pattern weft yarn which is woven on the underside of the fabric in this technique shows through the fabric surface and holds the rows of the fabric surface apart. This is accomplished by changing the harness combination from warp-faced to balanced for pattern weft *B*, and by a somewhat different selection of pattern weft yarns. Pattern weft *A* is twice the size of the warp in a color contrasting the warp. Pattern weft *B* is the size of the warp and is close to the warp in color. A gentle beat prevents the weft yarns from compacting too firmly. A sample woven in double weft Marsh appears in *Photo 12-1*. The Table of Harness Combinations and Treadling is given *(Figure 12-1A)*, as well as the diagram of the passage of weft yàrns *(Figure 12-1B)*.

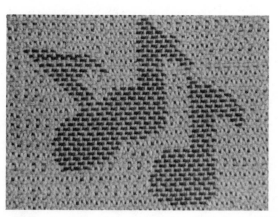

Ph. 12-1. Sample woven in double weft Marsh.

INSIGHTS

Why "Marsh"?

Chapter 12 involving double weft Marsh is a variation of Summer & Winter double weft, and was in need of a name to establish its identity. Since nothing in the weave structure suggested a unique title, I have selected a family name, "Marsh", for Elberta Hubbard Marsh, to whom this book is dedicated.

"The intent of all art is to communicate your feelings and emotions to another. Art has its rise in the need of human companionship. You feel certain thoughts and you strive to express them. You may express by music, by chiseled shapes, by painted canvas or by written words. At the last all art is one."

Elbert Hubbard

Weft Inlay For a Reversible Fabric

It is possible to weave a fabric which is reversible even though weft inlay yarns have been added in the piece. If the weft inlay area is designed with gradual curves, the weft inlay is carried only a short distance from row to row on the underside of the fabric. This small amount of carried weft may not show at all if the yarns are somewhat textured. The loops of the carried weft may also create an outline which is, in itself, an attractive addition to a piece. The front and back of a shawl woven in double weft Marsh are shown. The weft inlay area on the fabric surface is only slightly visible on the reverse side.

Weft inlay added to a design in double weft Marsh.

Reverse side of the above piece. The carried weft inlay yarns hardly show.

Weaving a Successful Border

The hand of a border and accompanying fabric must be compatible. The drape of the finished article should not be affected by the presence of the border area, and the visual effect of the two together must be pleasing. Colors which appear in the border should appear in the principal fabric. Narrow warp stripes involving one or two warp ends of a color used in the border are effective.

Double weft Marsh is a technique

Double weft Marsh.

Fig. 12-1A. Table of Harness Combinations and Treadling.

Row:	weft color:	Harness Combinations and Treadling:			
1	A	1 ←	OR →	1,2,4
	B	1 ←	OR →	1,2
2	A	3 ←	OR →	2,3,4
	B	3 ←	OR →	3,4

weft-faced · warp-faced · balanced

Fig. 12-1B. Side view of the passage of the pattern weft yarns.

Key:	Row:	weft color:	Passage of Pattern wefts:
pattern weft A	1	A	
		B	
pattern weft B		1,2	1,2,4
		3	3
	2	A	
		B	
		3,4	2,3,4

Thread double weft Marsh on harnesses 1,2,3,4, the same as double weft Summer & Winter. For a fabric with good drape, the warp should be a soft yarn comparable to 5/2 cotton in size, or finer. The sett is to square. For 5/2 cotton, the sett to square is 15 ends per inch.

Pattern weft *A*, the heavy weft yarn, is treadled in Row 1 exactly like double weft Summer & Winter. For areas in which pattern weft *A* is to be woven on the fabric surface, lift harness 1 (weft-faced). For areas in which it is to appear on the underside of the fabric, change the treadling and lift harnesses 1,2&4 (warp-faced). Pattern weft *B* follows, beginning at the same selvedge as pattern weft *A*. Where pattern weft *A* is woven warp-faced, lift harness 1 for pattern weft *B* (weft-faced), weaving it on the fabric surface. Where pattern weft *A* is woven weft-faced, lift harnesses 1&2 for pattern weft *B* (balanced). The change in weave structure occurs when harnesses 1&2 are lifted instead of the expected harnesses 1,2&4. Harness combination 1&2 is a balanced treadling which prevents pattern weft *A* from forming a totally weft-faced fabric surface.

In Row 2, begin with pattern weft *A*. Lift harness 3 for areas in which pattern weft *A* is to be woven on the fabric surface (weft-faced). In areas where it is to appear on the underside of the fabric, change the treadling and lift harnesses 2,3&4 (warp-faced). Pattern weft *B* follows. In areas where pattern weft *A* is woven warp-faced, lift harness 3 for pattern weft *B* (weft-faced). In areas where pattern weft *A* is woven weft-faced, lift harnesses 3&4 for pattern weft *B* (balanced). No ground weft is involved in double weft Marsh. Repeat these two rows for areas of the fabric which require treadling changes for design development.

For areas of the fabric which require no treadling changes within each row, treadle the appropriate weft-faced harness combination and throw the pattern weft shuttle selvedge-to-selvedge which is to be woven on the fabric surface. Then treadle the appropriate warp-faced or balanced harness combination and throw the second pattern weft shuttle selvedge-to-selvedge to appear on the underside of the fabric.

115

Weft Inlay

Weft inlay is an effective design tool with double weft Marsh and is added in the usual manner. Before weft inlay yarns are added, both pattern weft yarns of Row 1 and 2 are woven. In areas where weft inlay is to be added, treadle the warp-faced harness combination for pattern weft *A*, and the balanced harness combination for pattern weft *B*. Then treadle the appropriate weft-faced harness combination for that row and add the weft inlay yarns, entering and exiting the shed from the underside of the fabric as described in Chapter 2. A border for a skirt involving two areas of weft inlay is shown in *Photo 12-2.*

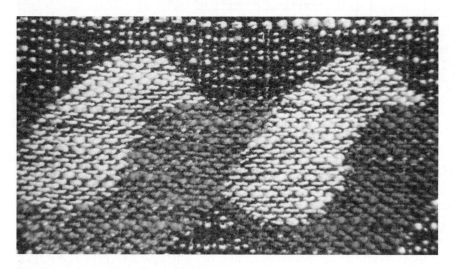

Ph. 12-2. Weft inlay added to double weft Marsh.

Suitable Projects

Double weft Marsh is a light weight firm material which drapes very well. It is suitable for a wide range of applications, including clothing, table linens, light weight blankets or throws, curtains, and borders for fabrics which are woven in either plain weave or twill. Refer to Appendix A for details.

well-suited to the weaving of border motifs. The warp yarns are visible in the freeform weave, and if one of the pattern weft yarns is close to the warp in color, good visual communication is created between the border and principal fabric. The pattern area involving two pattern weft yarns can be woven with the same hand as the principal fabric. In the photo of the border and fabric area of a shawl, notice the single warp thread of a different color which appears at regular intervals throughout the warp. This provides an additional communication between the colors in the border and body of the fabric. The treadling for the body of the fabric is a balanced broken twill, lifting harnesses 1&2, 3&4, 2&3, 4&1.

Enlargement of the border and fabric of a shawl woven in double weft Marsh.

"'Clack-clack' the loom cries a thousand times, but less than a foot is done." From *"The Liao-Ling Silk"*
Bai Juyi, T'ang Dynasty

(Left)
Ph. 12-3. Skirt and shawl worn as an ensemble.

(Below)
Ph. 12-4. Shawl, also woven of 5/2 and flake cotton, to be worn with the skirt.

(Left)
Ph. 12-5. Skirt woven of 5/2 and flake cotton. The body of the skirt is woven in balanced broken twill; the design motif of the border in double weft Marsh. Woven by the author.

13.

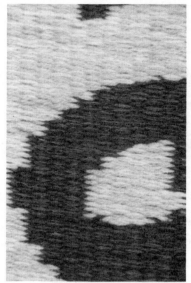

Broadweft Summer & Winter

Freeform Technique

Broadweft Summer & Winter and Collingwood's "shaft switching" method result in identical fabrics. The two methods of weaving, however, are totally different.

The threading for broadweft Summer & Winter is the same as other freeform Summer & Winter techniques, harnesses 1,2,3,4 repeated selvedge-to-selvedge. The warp should be of a strong two-ply yarn. 5/2 or 3/2 cotton, or a comparable size yarn in a cotton/linen blend, are good choices.

The warp is sett with fewer ends per inch than double weft Summer & Winter. The following chart gives the appropriate sett for warp yarns comparable to 5/2 and 3/2 cotton using different pattern weft yarns.

Warp Comparable To:	Sett	Weft Comparable To:
5/2 cotton	8 epi	3/12 wool and finer
5/2 cotton	5 epi	medium rug wool (600-1200 yards per pound)
3/2 cotton	4-5 epi	medium rug wool
3/2 cotton	4 epi	heavy rug wool (300-600 yards per pound)

A close-up of a tote bag is shown *(Photo 13-1)* for which a 5/2 cotton warp has been used. The sett is 8 ends per inch, with weft yarns comparable to a medium weight rug wool.

Broadweft Summer & Winter and Shaft Switching

"Shaft switching" is a technique developed by Peter Collingwood which has become very popular during the past few years. A device is added to a 4-harness loom which makes it possible to weave complex geometric figures in a weave structure identical to broadweft Summer & Winter. For the shaft switching method, warp ends which are threaded on harnesses 3 and 4 in traditional Summer & Winter are threaded instead through doup heddles. The doups are connected to levers which position each pattern warp end either with harness 3 or harness 4, depending on the design motif. Each pattern warp end is manipulated individually to form the warp- and weft-faced pattern areas of a piece, and levers must be changed each time the design lines are changed. For this reason, geometric designs are easier to weave than those involving curved lines.

It is also easier if the number of warp ends per inch is limited to fewer than 5.

Using the broadweft Summer & Winter technique, the same weave structure used in shaft switching can be woven with no loom adaptation. Both shaft switching and broadweft Summer & Winter are time-consuming techniques, but the broadweft method is generally quicker and less cumbersome.

Freeform Twill as a Broadweft Technique

Historically, there is evidence that double weft twill was woven as a broadweft twill using fewer warp ends per inch than are necessary to square the weave. The weave structure of twill is capable of compacting well, and weft yarns can easily be beaten to conceal the warp. Heavy, durable floor mats were woven in this fashion, often using reeds or supple young branches for the weft.

To weave double weft twill as a broadweft technique, sley the warp described in Chapter 10 for double weft twill at fewer ends per inch and use heavier pattern weft yarns. If the warp is a size comparable to 5/2 cotton, the sett should be 10 ends per inch. The pattern weft yarns should be twice the size of the warp.

Any of the treadling sequences for double weft twill can be used for broadweft twill. Because the pattern weft yarns compact in broadweft twill, and a diagonal line is therefore not clearly evident, the broken treadling sequence is a good choice. This treadling sequence is easier to follow, since the same pair of harness combinations is used for both pattern wefts A & B in each row. The Table of Harness Combinations and Treadling for the broken treadling sequence is repeated from Chapter 10.

I have not devoted an entire chapter to the weaving of broadweft twill because the technique involves the

Ph. 13-1. Close-up of a tote bag woven in broadweft Summer & Winter.

The harness combinations and treadling sequence for broadweft Summer & Winter are the same as double weft Summer & Winter. The Table of Harness Combinations and Treadling (Fig. 13-1A), and a diagram of the passage of pattern weft yarns (Fig. 13-1B) are given.

Row:	weft color:	Harness Combinations and Treadling:		
1	A	1 ←	OR →	1,2,4
	B	1 ←	OR →	1,2,4
2	A	3 ←	OR →	2,3,4
	B	3 ←	OR →	2,3,4
		weft-faced		warp-faced

Broadweft Summer & Winter.

Fig. 13-1A. Table of Harness Combinations and Treadling.

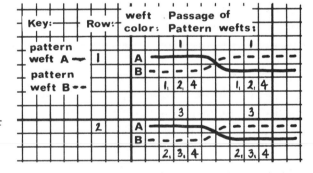

Fig. 13-1B. Side view of the passage of pattern weft yarns.

Two pattern weft yarns, A and B, are used for weaving broadweft Summer & Winter. They should be of comparable size to one another and in colors which contrast. The yarns should be of a suitable size to completely cover the warp yarns when beaten into place. No ground weft is involved.

The procedure for weaving broadweft Summer & Winter is the same as weaving double weft Summer & Winter. However, the resulting fabric looks totally different because the pattern weft yarns completely cover the warp yarns in the broadweft technique.

In Row 1, pattern wefts A and B use the same harness combinations: harness 1 (weft-faced), and harnesses 1,2&4 (warp-faced). Pattern weft A is woven first. For areas in which pattern weft A is woven on the fabric surface, lift harness 1. For areas in which it is to appear on the underside of the fabric, change the treadling and lift harnesses 1,2&4. Pattern weft B follows, starting at the same selvedge as pattern weft A. The same pair of harness combinations is used but in positions opposite pattern weft A. Where pattern weft A is woven warp-faced, lift harness 1 for pattern weft B (weft-faced). Where pattern weft A is woven weft-faced, lift harnesses 1,2&4 for pattern weft B (warp-faced).

Row 2 is woven in the same manner, but involves different harness combinations: harness 3 (weft-faced), and harnesses 2,3&4 (warp-faced). Pattern weft A is woven first. Lift harness 3 in areas in which pattern weft A is woven on the fabric surface. Change the treadling and lift harnesses 2,3&4 for areas in which pattern weft A appears on the underside of the fabric. Pattern weft B follows, using the same pair of harness combinations but in positions opposite pattern weft A. For areas in which pattern weft A is woven weft-faced, lift harnesses 2,3&4 for pattern weft B (warp-faced). For areas in which pattern weft A is woven warp-faced, lift harness 3 for pattern weft B (weft-faced). This two-row treadling sequence is repeated throughout areas of the fabric which involve treadling changes within each row.

In areas which involve no treadling changes, both pattern weft shuttles are woven selvedge-to-selvedge. Treadle the weft-faced harness combination and throw the pattern weft shuttle selvedge-to-selvedge which is to be woven on the fabric surface. Then treadle the appropriate warp-faced harness combination and throw the second pattern weft shuttle selvedge-to-selvedge, weaving on the underside of the fabric. Repeat this process for each row.

Weft Inlay

Before weft inlay yarns are added, both pattern weft yarns of Row 1 or 2 are woven first. For each pattern weft yarn, treadle the warp-faced harness combination in areas where weft inlay yarns are to be added. Then treadle the appropriate weft-faced harness combination and add the weft inlay yarns, entering and exiting the shed from the underside of the fabric, according to the method described in Chapter 2. It may be necessary to use a yarn slightly heavier than either pattern weft yarn for weft inlay since two pattern weft yarns pass through the inlay area.

Suitable Projects

Broadweft Summer & Winter results in a heavy, relatively unstable fabric which has considerable give and does not hold its shape well unless woven with a very firm weft yarn. Therefore, it is best to use this technique only for articles which involve minimal fabric stress. Rugs woven with stiff wool weft yarns are perhaps the best application. It is also possible to weave pillow covers or tote bags, but care must be taken to line the pieces and place the stress on the lining rather than the outer fabric. Refer to Appendix A for details.

same shortcomings as broadweft Summer & Winter. A ground weft cannot be added to broadweft twill and, while the pattern weft rows do compact well, the fabric lacks stability. Therefore, applications for the weave are limited. However, it does provide an appearance quite different from broadweft Summer & Winter, as shown in the following photograph.

Broadweft twill

Row:	Weft Color:	Harness Combinations:
1.	A,B	1-or-1,2,3
2.	A,B	3-or-1,3,4
3.	A,B	2-or-1,2,4
4.	A,B	4-or-2,3,4
	weft-faced	warp-faced

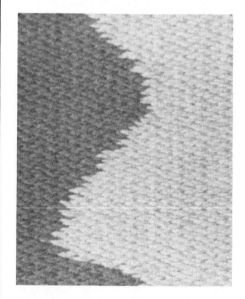

Sampler woven in broadweft twill.

"A great deal of the joy of life consists in doing perfectly, or at least to the best of one's ability, everything which he attempts to do. There is a sense of satisfaction, a pride in surveying such a work — a work which is rounded, full, exact, complete in all its parts. . . . It is this conscientious completeness which turns work into art. The smallest thing, well done, becomes artistic."

William Mathews

(Above)
Ph. 13-2. Sample woven in 5/2 Verel and medium weight wool. Woven by Elaine Lee.

(Right)
Ph. 13-3. Tote bag woven in 5/2 cotton and fine weight wool, using a design motif with curved lines. Woven by the author.

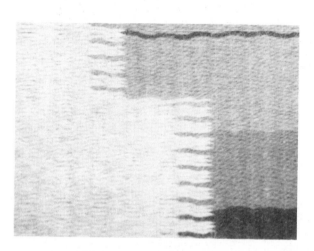

(Above)
Ph. 13-4. Wallhanging woven in 3/2 cotton and heavy weight wool with areas of weft inlay. Woven by Pat Short.

(Above left)
Ph. 13-5. Enlargement of an area of the wallhanging in Ph. 13-4 to show the feathered design edges.

(Below)
Ph. 13-6. Rug in 10/2 cotton and fine weight wool. Woven by the author.

(Left)
Ph. 13-7. Enlargement of one area of the rug in Ph. 13-6 to show the spaced feathering.

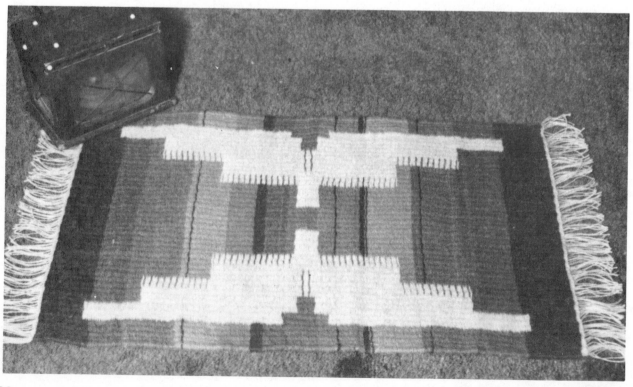

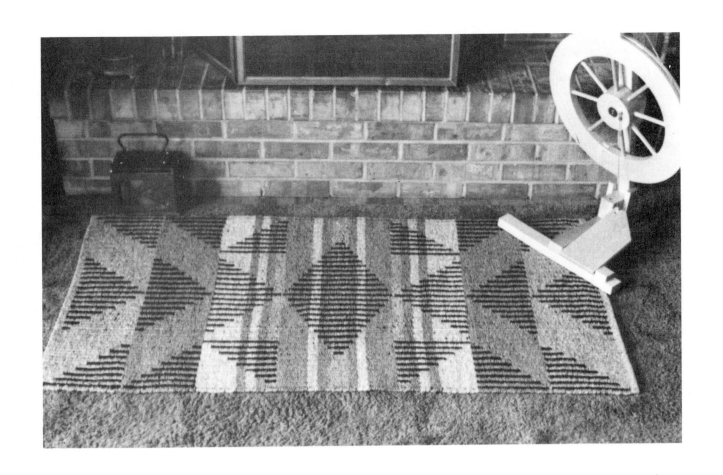

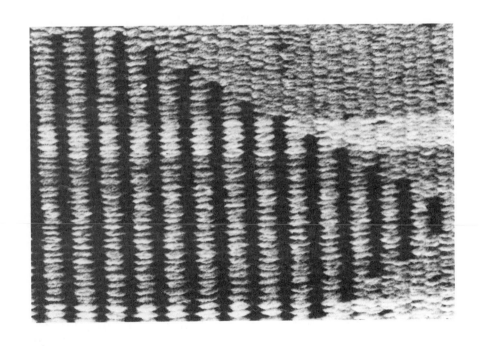

(Top)
Ph. 13-8. Rug in 5/2 cotton and medium weight wool. Woven by Ann Christensen.

(Bottom)
Ph. 13-9. Enlargement of one area of the rug shown in Ph. 13-8.

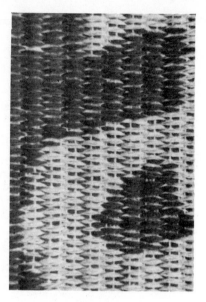

14.

Broadweft Ms & Os

Freeform Technique

Broadweft Ms & Os technique is similar to freeform Ms & Os woven with two pattern wefts. The threading is the same as freeform Ms & Os, harnesses 1,2,1,2,3,4,3,4 repeated selvedge-to-selvedge. For broadweft Ms & Os, use a strong 2-ply yarn of medium weight for the warp. 5/2 or 3/2 cotton is a good choice. The sett is fewer ends per inch than is necessary to square the weave. The following chart gives the appropriate sett for warp yarns comparable to 5/2 and 3/2 cotton using various sizes of yarn for weft.

Warp Comparable To:	Sett	Weft Comparable To:
5/2 cotton	8 epi	3/12 wool and finer
5/2 cotton	5 epi	medium rug wool (600-1200 yards per pound)
5/2 cotton	5 epi	heavy rug wool (300-600 yards per pound)
3/2 cotton	5 epi	medium rug wool
3/2 cotton	4-5 epi	heavy rug wool

The harness combinations are the same as freeform Ms & Os, although the treadling sequence is somewhat different. The Table of Harness Combinations and Treadling are given in *Figure 14-1A*, followed by a diagram of the passage of the pattern weft yarns *(Figure 14-1B)*. A sample woven in broadweft Ms & Os appears in *Photo 14-1.*

INSIGHTS

Broadweft Ms & Os Weave Structure

As with freeform Ms & Os, the two weave structures involved in broadweft Ms & Os are balanced (instead of weft-faced) and warp-faced. Because of the threading sequence used in freeform and broadweft Ms & Os, a balanced treadling permits the weft yarn to pass over a sufficient number of warp ends to create a long weft float covering the warp.

Broadweft Techniques Compared

A successful broadweft weave is one in which a ground weft can be added for stability and the pattern weft rows completely cover the warp and ground weft. Unfortunately, this is difficult to achieve. The two broadweft techniques presented, Ms & Os and Summer &

Winter, are as successful as any. Even so, neither technique totally fulfills both desired attributes.

The addition of a ground weft to broadweft freeform techniques is generally unstatisfactory, as the ground rows tend to keep the pattern weft rows separated. It is not possible to add ground weft to broadweft Summer & Winter without distorting the weave. The pattern weft passes over 3 warp ends and under 1 in Summer & Winter, which does not create a weft float of sufficient length to cover the warp. Because a ground weft cannot be added, broadweft Summer & Winter is not a stable weave. However, pattern weft rows compact sufficiently to cover the warp. The resulting fabric is heavy and durable, and is especially well-suited for rugs.

Ground weft can be added to broadweft Ms & Os, resulting in a firm weave. However, the pattern weft does not easily cover both the warp and ground weft, which prevents this weave from being totally weft-faced. Because pattern wefts pass over and under four warp ends, a fairly long weft float is created. If the pattern weft yarns are carefully selected, it is actually possible to cover the warp and ground weft, fulfilling both traits desirable in broadweft techniques. The resulting fabric is generally lighter in weight than broadweft Summer & Winter.

Pattern Weft Yarns For Broadweft Ms & Os

With the addition of a ground weft to broadweft Ms & Os, it is difficult for the weft-faced areas to completely cover the warp and ground weft. Therefore, it is best to use a pattern weft yarn which has the facility of a soft spun yarn to compact firmly and, at the same time, expand and fill the weft-faced areas. The yarn may, in fact, be a soft spun wool or cotton. Or it may be several finer yarns which are wound together on a bobbin.

Ph. 14-1. Sample woven in broadweft Ms & Os.

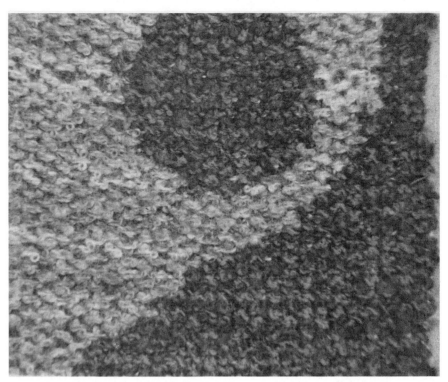

Broadweft Ms & Os.

Fig. 14-1A. Table of Harness Combinations and Treadling. "Balanced" is the same as "weft-faced" in freeform and double weft Ms & Os (left).

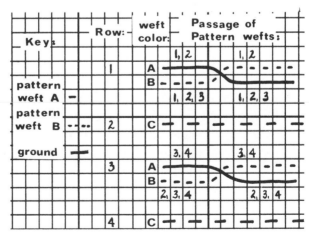

Fig. 14-1B. Side view of the passage of the pattern weft yarns (left).

Broadweft Ms & Os involves the use of two pattern weft yarns, *A* and *B*, which are the same weight as one another, and in colors which contrast one another and the warp. In addition to the pattern weft yarns, broadweft Ms & Os is woven with a ground weft which is the size and color of the warp, and may be the same as the warp.

In Row 1, the same pair of harness combinations is used for both pattern weft yarns, harnesses 1&2 (balanced), and harnesses 1,2&3 (warp-faced). In Row 1, pattern weft A is woven first. Lift harnesses 1&2 for those areas which are to be woven on the fabric surface (balanced). Change the treadling and lift harnesses 1,2&3 for areas in which pattern weft A appears on the underside of the fabric (warp-faced). The treadling is alternated between these two harness combinations as many times as the design dictates. Pattern weft B follows, starting at the same selvedge as pattern weft A, and using the same harness combinations as pattern weft A, but in opposite positions. In areas where pattern weft A is woven balanced, lift harnesses 1,2&3 for pattern weft B (warp-faced). In areas where pattern weft A is woven warp-faced, change the treadling and lift harnesses 1&2 for pattern weft B (balanced).

Row 2 is a ground row. Lift harnesses 1&3 and throw the shuttle selvedge-to-selvedge. No design is developed in the ground rows.

In Row 3, lift harnesses 3&4 in areas where pattern weft A is woven on the fabric surface (balanced). Change the treadling and lift harnesses 2,3&4 for areas in which pattern weft A appears on the underside of the fabric (warp-faced). Pattern weft B follows, using the same pair of harness combinations as pattern weft A, but in opposite positions. In areas where pattern weft A is woven balanced, lift harnesses 2,3&4 for pattern weft B (warp-faced). In areas where pattern weft A is woven warp-faced, lift harnesses 3&4 for pattern weft B (balanced).

Row 4 is a ground row involving no pattern development. Lift harnesses 2&4 and throw the shuttle selvedge-to-selvedge. This four-row treadling sequence is repeated in areas of the fabric in which treadling changes occur within each row.

In areas of the fabric involving no treadling changes, the two pattern weft shuttles in Row 1 and 3 are thrown selvedge-to-selvedge. Treadle the balanced harness combination and throw the pattern weft shuttle selvedge-to-selvedge which is to be woven on the fabric surface. Then throw the second pattern weft shuttle selvedge-to-selvedge, weaving on the underside of the fabric. The ground weft is thrown as usual, following each complete pattern weft row.

Weft Inlay

Both pattern weft shuttles of Rows 1 or 3 are woven before weft inlay yarns are added. For each pattern weft yarn of a row, treadle the warp-faced harness combination in areas where weft inlay yarns are to be added. Then treadle the appropriate balanced harness combination and add the weft inlay yarns, entering and exiting the shed from the underside of the fabric as described in Chapter 2.

Suitable Projects

The fabric woven in broadweft Ms & Os is extremely firm and drapes poorly. The fabric holds its shape well because of the ground weft. Items which are most suitable for broadweft Ms & Os include accessories, rugs, upholstery, wallhangings, and heavy outerwear involving no darts. Refer to Appendix A for details.

The Reverse Sides of Broadweft Ms & Os and Summer & Winter

Broadweft Summer & Winter is a reversible weave with well-defined design edges on both sides of the fabric.

Reverse side of fabric woven in broadweft Summer & Winter.

Broadweft Ms & Os is not as reversible a weave. Both pattern weft yarns are visible throughout the fabric, and the design is therefore not as clearly defined.

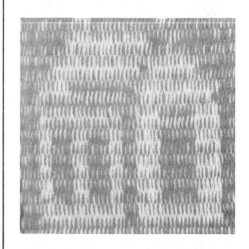

Reverse side of fabric woven in broadweft Ms & Os.

"Enthusiasm is a great hill climber."
Elbert Hubbard

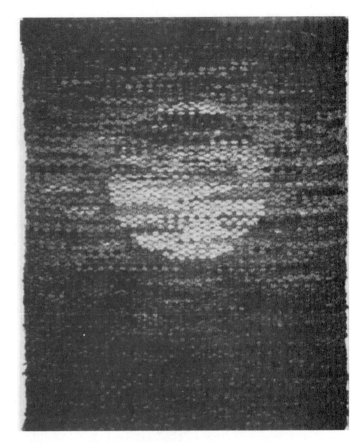

Ph. 14-2. "Industrial Sunrise", *a wallhanging woven in fine and medium weight wool. By the author.*

Ph. 14-3. "Violin" *woven of 5/2 cotton and medium weight wool. By Peggy MacArthur.*

Ph. 14-4. "Fish" *woven of 5/2 cotton and textured medium weight wool. By Agnes Galik.*

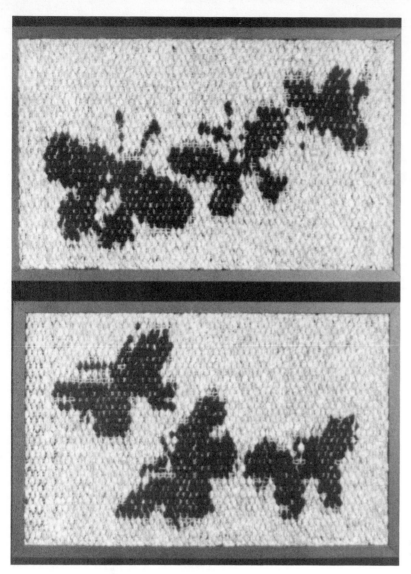

(Left)
Ph. 14-5. "Butterflies", a two-panel wall-hanging, is woven of 5/2 cotton and wool. Notice that the warp shows in several places as part of the design. Because the fabric is essentially broadweft, it is identified as such. By Joan Wells.

(Below)
Ph. 14-6. Sample woven of 5/2 cotton and fine weight wool. By Elaine Lee.

Ph. 14-7. Sample woven on 5/2 Verel and several fine weight wool yarns combined for each weft yarn. By the author.

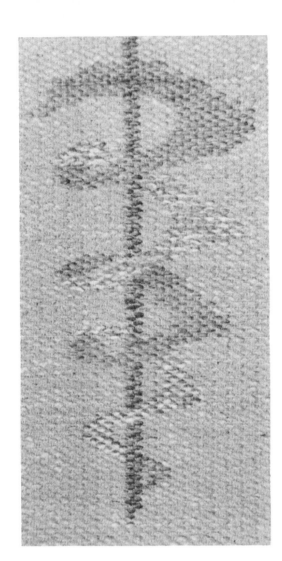

(Above)
Ph. 14-8. Framed hanging woven with 5/2 cotton and fine weight wool. Shading is achieved by combining several fine weft yarns for each pattern weft. Woven by Marcy Boettcher.

(Left)
Ph. 14-9. "Two bears" woven in 5/2 cotton and fine weight wool. The pattern weft used for the background involves two yarns of different colors. The blending of background colors allows the bear and tree motifs to predominate. Woven by Mae Matousek.

129

15.

Freeform Double Weave

Introduction

These final two double weft chapters, freeform double weave and freeform Finnweave, introduce new and quicker methods for weaving traditional double weave pick-up and Finnweave. Fabric woven in either technique looks the same as the traditional. Freeform double weave and Finnweave are classified with the freeform double weft techniques because each uses two pattern weft yarns. The preceding double weft techniques result in a single cloth, whereas freeform double weave and Finnweave involve the simultaneous weaving of two separate fabrics.

Freeform Technique

Freeform double weave involves upper and lower plain weave fabrics which connect in selected areas by changing positions with one another. In areas where the fabrics change position, a design in the lower warp is created as the upper fabric, and vice versa. *Photos 15-1* and *15-2* are of a piece woven in freeform double weave.

The warp for freeform double weave consists of two yarns of the same size and with the same stretch properties. The colors should sharply contrast one another. The number of warp ends is twice what is normally necessary to square the weave, since each layer of warp is woven independently to square for plain weave. The two warp yarns can be wound together on the warp board or reel and beamed as one warp.

INSIGHTS

Heritage of Double Weave

The technique of simultaneously weaving two plain weave fabrics and exchanging positions of the two fabrics at certain points to develop a pattern dates back many centuries. Evidence has been found in China indicating the presence of this technique as long ago as several centuries before the Christian era. The technique was also in common use in Persia, India, Russia, Peru, and the Scandinavian countries by the middle 1500s. The weave developed somewhat differently in each country, depending upon cultural influences, but all were derived from the basic double weave concept.

The heritage of freeform double weave in America is probably most notable in the weaving of coverlets. The coverlet woven in freeform double weave was more time-consuming to weave because two separate layers of fabric were involved, and additional yarns necessary to weave the coverlet raised the cost. The price for a coverlet woven in freeform double weave reflected the time and money invested and, as a result, few were woven. Those fortunate enough to own a coverlet woven in freeform double weave considered it a prized possession!

Use Freeform Double Weave For Block Designs

Either freeform double weave or freeform Finnweave can be used to weave design motifs involving solid block areas. The results are almost identical. If the piece is to be reversible, however, freeform double weave or reversible Finnweave must be used.

Freeform double weave is more suitable for area designs. Because the two warps alternate end-for-end in the threading, it is possible to develop clean design lines, both vertically and horizontally. Thin lines, however, are very difficult to weave with freeform double weave.

Ph. 15-1. Sampler woven in freeform double weave.

Ph. 15-2. Reverse side of the sample shown in Ph. 15-1.

The threading is harnesses 1,2,3,4 repeated selvedge-to-selvedge. One warp color is designated color A and is threaded on harnesses 1 and 3. The second warp color is designated color B and is threaded on harnesses 2 and 4. If the warp yarn being used squares at 15 epi (5/2 cotton, for instance), sley the warp for freeform double weave at 30 epi. When sleying the warp, it is best to have one of each color per dent. Therefore, with 30 epi, use a 15 dent reed and sley 2 per dent. If only a 12 dent reed is available, sley 2 warp ends in one dent, and 3 in the next.

The Table of Harness Combinations and Treadling (Fig. 15-1A), and a diagram of the passage of pattern weft yarns for freeform double weave (Fig. 15-1B) are given. Notice in Figure 15-1A, that the upper fabric is woven by treadling weft-faced harness combinations; the lower by treadling warp-faced harness combinations.

Row:	weft color:	Harness Combinations and Treadling:			
1	A	1 ←	OR →	1, 2, 4	
2	B	2 ←	OR →	1, 2, 3	
3	A	3 ←	OR →	2, 3, 4	
4	B	4 ←	OR →	1, 3, 4	
		weft-faced		warp-faced	
		(upper fabric)		(lower fabric)	

Freeform double weave.

Fig. 15-1A. Table of Harness Combinations and Treadling.

Fig. 15-1B. Diagram of the passage of pattern weft yarns.

Key:	Row:	weft color:	Passage of Pattern wefts:			
– pattern weft A —	1	A	1		2	
	2	B				
– pattern weft B --			1, 2, 3		1, 2, 4	
	3	A	3		4	
	4	B	1, 3, 4		2, 3, 4	

Photo 15-3 shows the portion of the sampler shown in *Photo 15-1* which will be used as the design motif to explain freeform double weave.

Ph. 15-3. Enlargement of one area of the sample shown in Ph. 15-1.

Two pattern weft yarns are necessary to weave freeform double weave, *A & B*. These two yarns are traditionally the same color and size as the warp yarns. The light-colored warp and weft in *Photo 15-3* are designated color *A*; the dark warp and weft, color *B*.

In Row 1, the two harness combinations involved are harness 1 for weft-faced areas (upper fabric), and harnesses 1,2&4 for warp-faced areas (lower fabric). Begin the shuttle at the left selvedge using pattern weft *A*. Lift harness 1, since pattern weft *A* is woven as the upper fabric at the left selvedge (weft-faced). The shuttle travels in this shed to the point where the treadling changes. At that point, lift harnesses 1,2&4, weaving pattern weft *A* as the lower fabric (warp-faced). Where pattern weft *A* is again woven as the upper fabric, change the treadling and lift harness 1 (weft-faced). Take the shuttle to the right selvedge.

The harness combinations for Row 2 involve harness 2 for weft-faced areas (upper fabric), and harnesses 1,2&3 for warp-faced areas (lower fabric). In Row 2, pattern weft *B* is woven in positions opposite pattern weft *A*. Begin the pattern weft *B* shuttle at the left selvedge. Because pattern weft *A* is woven weft-faced at the left selvedge, lift harnesses 1,2&3 for pattern weft *B* (warp-faced). The shuttle travels in that shed to the point where pattern weft *A* changes and is woven warp-faced. At that point, lift harness 2 for pattern weft *B* (weft-faced). Where pattern weft *A* is again woven weft-faced, change the treadling and lift harnesses 1,2&3 for pattern weft *B* (warp-faced). The shuttle travels in this shed to the right selvedge.

Row 3 is woven in the same manner as Row 1. With pattern weft *A*, lift harness 3 for weft-faced areas (upper fabric), and harnesses 2,3&4 for areas to be woven warp-faced (lower fabric). With the shuttle at the right selvedge, lift harness 3, since pattern weft *A* is woven as the upper fabric at the right selvedge (weft-faced). The shuttle travels through the shed to the point where the design changes. At that point, lift harnesses 2,3&4 (warp-faced), weaving pattern weft *A* as the lower fabric. Where the design dictates another treadling change, lift harness 3, weaving pattern weft *A* as the upper fabric (weft-faced). Take the shuttle to the left selvedge.

Pattern weft *B* is used in Row 4, and is woven in positions opposite pattern weft *A*. The harness combinations involved are harness 4 for weft-faced areas (upper fabric), and harnesses 1,3&4 for warp-faced areas (lower fabric). Beginning at the right selvedge, lift harnesses 1,3&4 for pattern weft *B* (warp-faced), since pattern weft *A*

Stripes in Freeform Double Weave

While freeform double weave is usually woven with only two colors in the warp and weft, it is possible to enhance a design by changing colors in one weft or by using stripes in one warp. When considering the use of stripes in freeform double weave, a good rule of thumb is to use stripes in the warp and/or weft of only one of the fabric layers. The second warp and weft should be one solid color. The solid area helps to emphasize the design areas and avoids visual confusion. A freeform double weave piece is shown which is woven traditionally with each fabric in solid color.

Freeform double weave butterfly woven traditionally using one color for each fabric layer.

A few rows of different colors and texture added to the weft of one fabric livens the design significantly.

Stripes added in the weft of one fabric layer to create design interest.

Trim Edges for Finnweave and Double Weave

The edges of fabrics woven in freeform double weave and Finnweave look best when none of the lower fabric extends beyond the upper fabric at either selvedge. Because both warps are usually wound with the same number of ends, it is inevitable that the lower fabric will extend by one or two warp ends at one selvedge. To solve the problem, remove the one extra lower warp end from double weave; the extra pair of lower warp ends in Finnweave.

Turned edge of Finnweave piece to show upper warp extended.

Keep the Fabrics Separate

Freeform double weave and Finnweave consist of two plain weave fabrics woven one on top of the other. When the upper and lower fabric shuttles are at the same selvedge, a question arises whether or not to interlock the edges. It is usually best to leave the sides open to allow the fabric to adjust and lay flat when the piece is off the loom. In order to leave the selvedges free of one another, make certain that the two weft yarns do not twist.

is woven weft-faced at the right selvedge. The shuttle travels to the point where pattern weft *A* is woven warp-faced. At that point, change the treadling and lift harness 4 for pattern weft *B* (weft-faced). Where pattern weft *A* changes treadling and is again woven weft-faced, lift harnesses 1,3&4 for pattern weft *B* (warp-faced). The shuttle travels to the left selvedge.

These four rows are repeated throughout the weaving in areas involving treadling changes within the rows. When the design line changes, it always changes in Rows 1 and 3 when weaving with pattern weft *A*. In Rows 2 and 4, pattern weft *B* completes whatever design is established with pattern weft *A*.

Both pattern weft shuttles are thrown selvedge-to-selvedge in areas of the fabric which do not involve treadling changes with the rows. In Row 1 using pattern weft *A*, lift harness 1 (weft-faced) if pattern weft *A* is to be woven as the upper fabric, and harnesses 1,2&4 (warp-faced) if it is to be woven as the lower fabric. Throw the shuttle selvedge-to-selvedge. For Row 2 using pattern weft *B*, treadle the appropriate harness combination to weave pattern weft *B* as the fabric layer opposite pattern weft *A*. Throw the shuttle selvedge-to-selvedge. For Row 3 using pattern weft *A*, lift harness 3 if Row 1 is woven weft-faced; harnesses 2,3&4 if Row 1 is woven warp-faced. Throw the shuttle selvedge-to-selvedge. In Row 4 using pattern weft *B*, lift harness 4 if Row 2 is woven weft-faced, and harnesses 1,3&4 is Row 2 is woven warp-faced. Throw the shuttle selvedge-to-selvedge.

Weft Inlay

Weft inlay is a row-by-row consideration in freeform double weave. For any of the 4 rows of freeform double weave, the pattern weft yarn passes through areas for which weft inlay is to be added treadling the warp-faced harness combination. When the pattern weft yarn has reached the far selvedge, lift the appropriate weft-faced harness for the row and add the weft inlay yarns, entering and exiting the shed from the underside of the fabric as described in Chapter 2.

Suitable Projects

Freeform double weave results in a reversible fabric which is of medium weight. However, the fabric does not drape well because of the two layers of weave. Suitable projects include accessories, table linens, rugs, wallhangings, and heavy vests which require no darts. Refer to Appendix A for details.

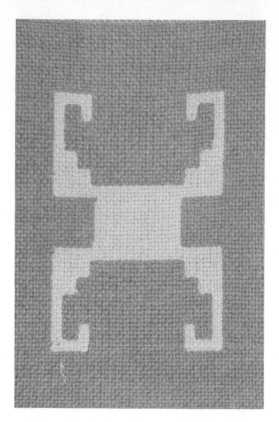

Ph. 15-4. Sampler in 5/2 Verel, woven by Lynn Moore.

Ph. 15-5. Sampler in 5/2 Verel, woven by Ann Christensen.

Ph. 15-7. Purse involving a repeated design, woven in fine weight wool. One warp and weft involve different colors. This provides an interesting contrast to the solid areas created by the second warp and weft which are the same color. Courtesy of June Mack.

Ph. 15-6. Needle case, woven in fine weight wool. Courtesy of June Mack.

Ph. 15-8. Purse in which one warp and weft are of a single light color, providing a solid background. The second warp is striped and the weft follows the same color sequence as the warp, creating solid design areas in alternating colors. Courtesy of June Mack.

16.

Freeform Finnweave

Introduction

Finnweave is a form of freeform double weave which has long been known to Scandinavian weavers. Traditionally, the weaving of Finnweave is a lengthy and somewhat confusing process involving one or two pick-up sticks. Using the technique of freeform design, it is possible to weave Finnweave quite simply with no pick-up sticks. *Photo 16-1* shows a traditional delicate Finnweave motif.

Ph. 16-1. Traditional Finnweave.

INSIGHTS

Finnweave Heritage

Finnweave is a variation of freeform double weave, in which two-thread horizontal and vertical lines are used to create delicate symmetrical designs. This freeform double weave technique was in use by the 13th Century in the Scandinavian countries, particularly in Sweden, and was called Dubbelväv (double weave). The name Finnväv (Finnweave) and Ryssväv (Russian weave) appear in documents of that time. The name currently used to describe this particular double weave is "Finnweave", although Finland is not necessarily the origin of the technique. A contemporary piece woven in Finnweave is shown in which the horizontal lines at the top of the design are feathered, while those lines along the sides and bottom are solid. Notice that the same variety of horizontal lines has been used for the outline of the fleur-de-lis. The design utilizes the block, as well as horizontal and vertical lines. The variety of line and block in design motifs is typical of Finnweave pieces woven throughout the past seven centuries.

Fleur-de-lis design woven in freeform Finnweave. The edges of the design involve both feathered and solid edge techniques.

Finishing Stitch

The following finishing stitch is an excellent one for pieces which are to have fringe, and will hold the edge equally as well as knots. Place the piece, right side up, on a lap board or other small working surface, with the edge to be worked facing you.

1)Cut a piece of warp thread 3 times the length of the edge to be stitched. This is the "edging thread". Thread the edging thread through a large eye needle. 2)With the edging thread, and working from right to left, start the first stitch by following the last row of weaving for 2", ending at the left selvedge. 3)Make a loop with the edging thread. The loop comes toward you from left to right, and lies on top of the fringe. 4)Counting three warp threads to the right, take the needle down through the fringe,

There are two types of Finnweave, reversible and nonreversible. Since the nonreversible method affords the weaver more design versatility, this technique is presented. The reverse side of the traditional Finnweave of *Photo 16-1* is shown in *Photo 16-2*. The nonreversibility of the weave is clearly evident!

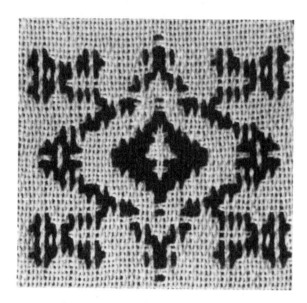

Ph. 16-2. Reverse side of the piece shown in Photo 16-1.

Freeform Finnweave

The warp for Finnweave is prepared like freeform double weave. Two strongly contrasting colored yarns the same size are wound and beamed together. Traditionally, a dark color is selected as color *A* (background), and a light color as color *B* (pattern). Each color warp forms a separate fabric layer which means that the total number of warp ends will be twice what is required to square either warp for plain weave. For 5/2 cotton, which is sett at 15 epi to square, 30 epi are necessary for the Finnweave warp.

The warp is threaded on harnesses 1,2,3,4. Color *A* (background) is threaded on harnesses 1 and 2. Color *B* (pattern) is threaded on harnesses 3 and 4. If possible, sley the two color *A* warp ends together and the two color *B* warp ends together. For 5/2 cotton, using a 15 dent reed, sley two ends per dent.

Two pattern weft yarns of different colors are necessary for weaving freeform Finnweave. These are traditionally the same colors as the two warp yarns, *A* and *B*. Rows 1 and 2 are woven with pattern weft *A*; Rows 3 and 4 with pattern weft *B*.

The process for weaving Finnweave is identical to freeform double weave. However, the four pairs of harness combinations must be changed to accommodate the different order of threading and treadling. The Table of Harness Combinations and Treadling is given in *Figure 16-1*.

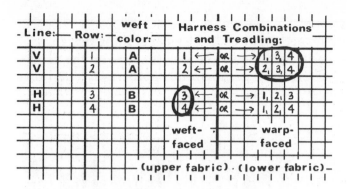

Line:	Row:	weft color:	Harness Combinations and Treadling:			
V	1	A	1 ← OR →	(1,3,4)		
V	2	A	2 ← OR →	(2,3,4)		
H	3	B	(3) OR →	1,2,3		
H	4	B	(4) ← OR →	1,2,4		
			weft-faced		warp-faced	
			(upper fabric)		(lower fabric)	

Fig. 16-1. Freeform Finnweave: Table of Harness Combinations and Treadling.
Harness combinations which form the design are circled.

The pattern in Finnweave is created with the lower pattern warp (color *B*). For areas involving design, the pattern warp threaded on harnesses 3&4 is brought up through the background warp, and is woven as the upper fabric.

Three design components are possible in Finnweave: the vertical line, horizontal line, and the solid block.

The *vertical line* involves two adjacent pattern warp ends, and is formed by a single pair of lower pattern warp threads. It is created in Rows 1 and 2 when treadling the warp-faced harness combinations which are circled in *Figure 16-1*, harnesses 1,3&4 or 2,3&4. The vertical line is two warp ends wide (unless a block is being formed) because pairs of background warp ends separate the pairs of pattern warp ends. The vertical line is automatically carried through the weaving of Rows 3 and 4.

The *horizontal line* is formed in Rows 3 and 4 by two adjacent pattern weft *B* rows. The line is created when treadling the weft-faced harness combinations which are circled in *Figure 16-1*, harness 3 or 4.

The *solid block* is woven by combining horizontal and vertical lines. The block begins with a horizontal line created in Rows 3 and 4. Then, in Rows 1 and 2, vertical lines are developed the length of the horizontal line. The block is thus developed, alternating horizontal and vertical lines, ending with a horizontal line. *Photo 16-3* shows each of the three design components as it is woven.

Ph. 16-3. The three design components for freeform Finnweave.

In place of a cartoon, the design for freeform Finnweave is developed on graph paper. The graph for the Finnweave piece in *Photo 16-1* is given in *Figure 16-2*.

under the three warp threads, from right to left, and bring the needle up. Make certain that the needle comes up through the loop. 5)Pull gently on the edging thread, securing the knot against the last row of weaving. 6)To the immediate right of the knot, and three rows back from the edge of the weaving, take the needle down through the weaving. 7)Bring the needle toward you under the weaving, and up at the weaving edge, still to the immediate right of the knot. 8) Pull edging thread into position, but do not pull so taut as to distort the weave.

The needle and edging thread are now in position to begin the second knot with step 3). Work steps 3)-8) until the edging thread has reached the right selvedge. Secure the thread with an inconspicuous knot, and weave the end back in. Clip the ends.

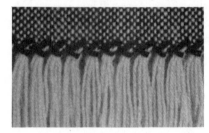

Stitched edge

Beginning the finishing stitch.

Finishing stitch in progress.

Counting Pairs of Pattern Warp in Freeform Finnweave

When counting pairs of pattern warp ends in freeform Finnweave, remember that only the bottom warp is involved in the counting. The top warp serves as background and is not involved. The following Photo shows a Finnweave warp in which harnesses 3 and 4 are lifted to count pairs of pattern warp ends.

Finnweave with harnesses 3 and 4 raised.

When it is necessary to take careful note of design placement, such as the beginning of the broad motif in Sequence 4 of Figure 16-2, it is wise to lift harnesses 3 and 4, count and mark the areas of design. The middle horizontal line in Sequence 4 involves 5 pairs of lower pattern warp, numbers 1-3 including right and left of center. With harnesses 3 and 4 lifted, place pins in the fabric to mark the outside pairs. The two horizontal lines to right and left of center involve warp pairs 8-10, and 14-16, respectively. Mark the outer pairs of each of these horizontal lines. Once the design lines are marked, drop harnesses 3 and 4 and weave Sequence 4.

It is not necessary to mark the design outline before weaving each sequence. This is done only when a design is initiated or altered considerably. The lower pattern warp may easily be viewed through the upper warp and the pairs of pattern warp ends counted as the shuttle is maneuvered through each shed.

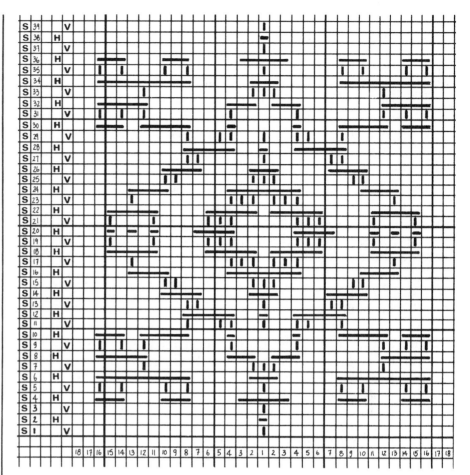

Fig. 16-2. Graph for the design woven in Photo 16-1.

Notice the "H"s and "V"s at the left of the graph. Each "H" represents the two rows in which horizontal lines are developed, Rows 3 and 4. Each "V" represents Rows 1 and 2 in which vertical lines are developed. A pair of rows which forms an "H" or "V" is referred to as a "Sequence". Notice also that horizontal and vertical lines are used in the squares of the design to indicate which type of line is woven. Each square in the graph represents two warp ends of pattern warp B which are lifted to create a vertical line, or two weft rows.

Only the pairs of pattern warp (color B) are indicated in the design graph; background warp (color A) is not included. Omission of the background warp allows the graph to be in proportion to the woven design. The background warp is woven *underneath* the pattern warp in design areas. Including it in the graph would therefore result in a design which appears twice as wide as it actually is. All four of the pattern weft rows are included in the graph, however, since design is developed in each row.

Before beginning to weave, it is helpful to lift all of pattern warp B (harnesses 3 and 4) and mark the center of the pattern warp. The pattern warp comes up through the background warp in pairs. Locate the center pair of pattern warp ends and place a pin in the weaving to mark the center. There are 35 pairs of pattern warp ends involved in the design shown in *Figure 16-2*. Because the design is symmetrical, the pairs can be numbered from the center out.

Weaving begins with Sequence 1 (S1) at the bottom of the graph.

According to the graph in *Figure 16-2*, the design begins with a vertical line. Therefore, the treadling begins with Rows 1 and 2, using pattern weft *A*. Lift harness 1. This weft-faced harness combination is *not* circled on *Figure 16-1* and is, therefore, background treadling. Move the shuttle through the shed until the center pair of pattern warp ends (lower warp) is reached. Change the treadling, lifting harnesses 1,3&4 (warp-faced), and weave under the one pair of pattern warp ends. The warp-faced harness combination *is* circled in *Figure 16-1*, indicating that pattern is being developed. According to the graph in *Figure 16-2*, only the one center pair of pattern warp ends is woven. Change the treadling back to harness 1 (background), and take the shuttle to the opposite selvedge.

Row 2 of Sequence 1 is also woven with pattern weft *A*, and completes the design started in Row 1. Lift harness 2 (background), and move the shuttle through to the center of the shed. Change the treadling and lift harnesses 2,3&4 (pattern) to accommodate the same pair of warp ends as Row 1. Change the treadling back to harness 2 (background), and weave to the opposite selvedge.

Next on the graph in *Figure 16-2* is Sequence 2 (S2). This is a horizontal sequence involving Rows 3 and 4 and pattern weft *B*. Only a vertical line is developed in Sequence 2. Therefore, it is not necessary to change the treadling within the rows, since no horizontal line is developed, and vertical lines are carried automatically through the horizontal rows. Lift harnesses 1,2&3 in the first row of Sequence 2 for background (Row 3), and harnesses 1,2&4 in the second row (Row 4). The shuttle travels selvedge-to-selvedge in each row.

Sequence 3 (S3) is woven exactly as Sequence 1, accommodating the center pair of pattern warp ends to continue the development of the vertical line.

Sequence 4 (S4) involves Rows 3 and 4 and the development of horizontal lines. Since the outermost blocks of the design motif are developed in this sequence, it is a good idea to lift pattern harnesses 3 and 4 to mark the placement of the horizontal lines. The procedure for locating and marking the pairs of lower pattern warp ends is presented in *INSIGHTS* on page 139. Pattern weft *B* is used.

In the first row of Sequence 4 (Row 3), lift harnesses 1,2&3 (background) and move the shuttle to the beginning of the first horizontal line (the 16th pair of pattern warp ends from the center). Change the treadling and lift harness 3 (pattern). Move the shuttle through that shed to the end of the first horizontal line (3 pairs of pattern warp ends). Change the treadling back to harnesses 1,2&3 (background) and move the shuttle to the next horizontal line. Change the treadling again to harness 3 (pattern), and move the shuttle through the shed to the end of that horizontal line (pairs 8-10). Change the treadling and lift harnesses 1,2&3 (background) and move the shuttle through this shed to the center horizontal line (pair 3 of pattern warp ends). Lift harness 3 and weave the center horizontal line (from pair 3 on one side of center to pair 3 on the other). Continue weaving across the row, alternating harnesses 1,2&3 for background and harness 3 for pattern areas. The second half of the row is woven exactly like the first half.

When developing a horizontal line in Rows 3 and 4, make certain to enter and exit the weft-faced shed to include the outside pair of pattern warp ends. The pair of background warp ends to either side of the outermost pair of pattern warp ends should not be included,

140

The Development of Horizontal Lines in Finnweave

The concept of developing the horizontal and vertical lines in Finnweave is confusing, at best. Placing additional attention upon development of the horizontal line may be helpful. The single horizontal line is developed in Rows 3 and 4. A solid block motif is developed using a horizontal line (Rows 3 and 4) at the beginning and end of a block. The following graph shows the method of creating a solid block and developing a single horizontal line.

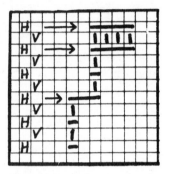

Horizontal lines developed in horizontal Rows 3 and 4.

If a block begins and ends with vertical Rows 1 and 2, or if a horizontal line is developed in the vertical rows, the result is quite different. The following graph shows what happens if the horizontal lines are developed in vertical Rows 1 and 2.

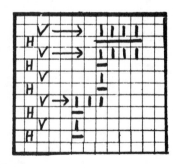

Horizontal lines developed in vertical Rows 1 and 2.

The lines created in Sequences 4, 8, and 10 are vertical and will be woven much as they appear in the graph. They will not connect into a horizontal line. When a block begins or ends with vertical rows, that edge will be feathered, not solid.

Nonreversible Finnweave is most effective when used for weaving linear designs. Two warp ends of the same color are threaded side-by-side, and two weft rows are woven consecutively using the same color. Therefore, it is possible to develop a two-thread vertical design line or two-thread horizontal design line with no difficulty. The "E" photographed from a "Noel" banner is a good example of a Finnweave design which would be difficult to weave using the freeform double weave technique.

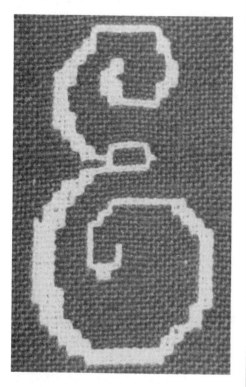

The "E" from a "Noel" banner woven in freeform Finnweave.

"And what is it to work with love? "It is to weave the cloth with threads drawn from your heart, even as your beloved were to wear the cloth." The Prophet *Kahil Gibran*

or the horizontal line will be extended beyond the desired length.

The second row of Sequence 4 (Row 4) completes the design motifs begun in the first row (Row 3). Lift harnesses 1,2&4 for background areas where harnesses 1,2&3 were lifted in Row 3. Lift harness 4 for the pattern areas where harness 3 was lifted in Row 3.

Sequence 5 (S5) involves Rows 1 and 2 and the development of vertical lines. Lift harness 1 (background) for Row 1 of Sequence 5 and weave with pattern weft *A* to the first vertical line (the 16th pair of pattern warp ends, counting from the center). Change the treadling and lift harnesses 1,3&4 (pattern) to accommodate just the 16th pair of pattern warp ends. Change the treadling to harness 1 (background) for one pair of pattern warp ends, and back to harnesses 1,3&4 (pattern) to accommodate the 14th pair of pattern warp ends (counting from the center). Continue changing the treadling in this manner, accommodating the appropriate pairs of pattern warp ends according to the design graph.

Row 2 of Sequence 5 is woven like Row 1, accommodating the same pairs of pattern warp ends to form vertical lines. Lift harness 2 for background areas, and harnesses 2,3&4 for pattern areas.

Sequences 6 through 39 are woven in the same manner as Sequences 1 through 5. Once the design lines are established in Sequence 5, subsequent changes in the design will be easier to follow.

The two pattern wefts are thrown selvedge-to-selvedge for areas in which no treadling changes occur. The background warp (harnesses 1&2) forms the upper fabric, and the pattern warp (harnesses 3&4) forms the lower fabric. The treadling for each of the 4 rows in *Figure 16-1* is the harness combination which is *not* circled. Lift harness 1 in Row 1, followed by harness 2 in Row 2, both using pattern weft *A*. In Row 3, lift harnesses 1,2&3, followed by harnesses 1,2&4 in Row 4, both using pattern weft *B*.

Weft Inlay

Weft inlay is possible with freeform Finnweave, but is not presented. The design in Finnweave is effective by itself and is not easily enhanced by the addition of different weft yarns or by warp stripes. If the addition of weft inlay yarns is desired, follow the instructions given for freeform double weave in the preceding chapter.

Suitable Projects

Fabric woven in freeform Finnweave is medium weight, not reversible, and drapes moderately well. Projects which are suitable are the same as freeform double weave, and include accessories, table linens, rugs, wallhangings, and vests which require no darts. Refer to Appendix A for details.

In addition to the above, because of the nature of the designs for freeform Finnweave, small weavings involving a single design motif are attractive for note cards, ornaments, and pockets or inserts for clothing. Borders for skirts, jackets and coats may also be woven in Finnweave. In this case, the border area requires a short warp for only that area. The body of the fabric is then woven in plain weave, using only the background (top) warp threaded on harnesses 1 and 2.

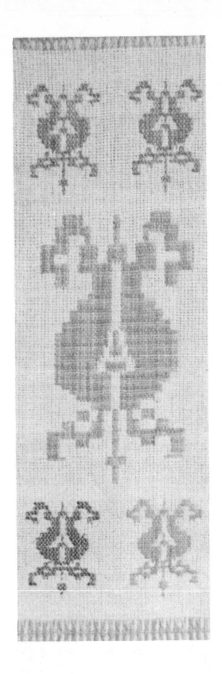

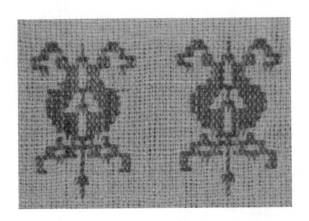

(Top left)
Ph. 16-4. Traditional Finnweave design motif woven in linen, in which the lower fabric warp and weft have been space dyed. Woven by Birgit Barron.

(Top right)
Ph. 16-5. Asymmetrical bird motif of medium weight wool. Woven by the author.

(Center)
Ph. 16-6. Enlargement of one area of wallhanging by Birgit Barron shows the delicacy of the design.

(Right)
Ph. 16-7. Symmetrical Finnweave design woven in 5/2 cotton. By Dian Zahner.

142

(Right)
Ph. 16-8. A small design motif to be used as an appliqué for a skirt. Woven in 5/2 cotton by Betty Johannesen.

(Below left)
Ph. 16-9. Holiday banner woven in 5/2 cotton, which demonstrates the versatility of the technique. Woven by Birgit Barron.

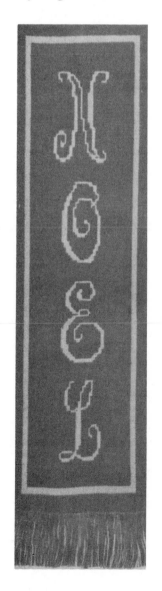

(Right)
Ph. 16-10. Small hanging woven in medium weight wool. By Freddie Ingebrigtser.

(Above)
Ph. 16-11. Small delicate design motif. Woven by the author.

Appendices

Appendix A
Projects Most Appropriate
for Each Freeform Design Technique

FABRIC WEIGHT	ARTICLE	SECTION I FREEFORM TECHNIQUES								SECTION II DOUBLE WEFT			BROAD-WEFT		FREEFORM	
		TWILL	OVERSHOT	SUMMER & WINTER	Ms & Os	HUCK	LACE HUCK	BRONSON LACE	BROCADE	TWILL	SUMMER & WINTER	MARSH	SUMMER & WINTER	Ms & Os	DOUBLE WEAVE	FINN-WEAVE
CLOTHING																
M or H	CAPE, COAT, RUANA				X	X			X	X						
M or H	VEST				X	X			X	X				X		
M	VEST SUITINGS					X					X	X			X	X
M	PURSE/TOTE	X	X	X	X	X			X	X	X			X	X	X
L	SKIRT, SLACKS DRESS, BLOUSE	X					X	X	X			X				
L or M	BORDER with fabric woven in: Plain Weave		X	X			X	X			X	X				X
L or M	BORDER with fabric woven in: Twill			X					X	X	X	X				
LINENS																
L or M	PLACEMAT RUNNER	X	X	X	X	X	X	X		X	X	X			X	X
L	TABLECLOTH FINGERTIP TOWEL	X					X	X								
HOUSEHOLD																
H	RUG				X					X			X	X	X	X
M-H	UPHOLSTERY PILLOW				X	X							X	X	X	X
M	BEDSPREAD UPHOLSTERY PILLOW	X	X	X	X	X			X	X						
M	BLANKET THROW	X					X	X		X	X					
L	DRAPE CURTAIN	X	X				X	X	X			X				
ALL WEIGHTS	WALLHANGING	X	X	X	X	X	X	X	X	X	X	X	X	X	X	X

FABRIC WEIGHT	WARP SIZE	EPI	SETT & BEAT	WEFT	DRAPE
Light (L)	5/2 cc* & finer	16-80	To square	Same as warp.	Excellent
Medium (M)	5/2 cc to medium rug wool	8-18	To square	Same as warp to twice the size.	Good
Medium-Heavy (M-H)	5/2 cc to medium rug wool	6-12	Fewer than necessary to square. Firm beat.	2 - 4 times warp size.	Fair
Heavy (H)	3/2 cc to medium rug wool	4-10	Half of what is necessary to square, or fewer. Firm beat resulting in a double thick fabric.	4 - 5 times warp size.	Poor to very poor

*cc — cotton count

146

Appendix B
Setts for Commonly Used Reeds

SLEY

Warp ends per dent	Reed size (dents per inch)			
	8	**10**	**12**	**15**
1, (skip)	4	5	6	7 1/2
1	8	10	12	15
1,1,2	10 2/3	13 1/3	16	20
1,2	12	15	18	22 1/2
1,2,2	13 1/3	16 2/3	20	25
2	16	20	24	30
2,2,3	18 2/3	23 1/3	28	35
2,3	20	25	30	37 1/2
2,3,3	21 1/3	26 2/3	32	40
3	24	30	36	45

ENDS PER INCH

NOTES:
— 1 or 2 ends per dent is ideal.

— 3 ends per dent works, but stripes may occur in fabric.

— when mixing numbers of ends per dent, use adjacent numbers in sleying (1,2; 2,3; or 2,3,3).

— stripes are created by using 3 numbers in the arrangement of warp ends in the reed: 1,2,3 instead of 2,2,2; or by using 2 numbers not adjacent: 3,1 instead of 2,2.

Appendix C
Yards Per Pound for Natural Yarns

YARN SIZE

Yarn	1	3/1	3/2	5/1	5/2	10/1	10/2	20/1	20/2	40/1	40/2	80/1	80/2
Linen	300	900	450	1500	750	3000	1500	6000	3000	12000	6000	24000	12000
Cotton/Silk	840	2520	1260	4200	2100	8400	4200	16800	8400	33600	16800	67200	33600
Wool	560	1680	840	2800	1400	5600	2800	11200	5600	22400	11200	44800	22400

Factory Count is the number 1 size of each yarn and
is the largest size of the yarn.
linen — 300 yards per pound
cotton/silk — 840 yards per pound
wool — 560 yards per pound
The top number of a yarn equation is the **size;** the
bottom number the **ply.** For 20/2 cotton, the yarn
is size 20, and 2 yarns are plyed together (2-ply).

To find the number of yards per pound for a yarn
given the factory count:

Factory count	x	size	÷	ply	=	yards per pound
Cotton: 840	x	20	÷	2	=	5600 yards per pound

There are 5600 yards in one pound of 20/2 cotton.

Note:
The larger the number for yarn size,
the finer the yarn.

For warp strength, it is generally advisable to
select a 2-ply yarn rather than one with a
single ply.

Notes:

The card is printed on 110# index stock (medium weight.)

It measures 5x8 and fits into a 5x8 file box.

Print 1/2 of the cards with the graph on the left;
the other half with the graph on the right.
This helps distribute the bulk of the samples.

Place a small sample on the record card with
weaving information.
Large samples can be filed in manilla folders in another box.

In addition to woven samples and information, record:
— samples from newsletters
— photos of fabrics from weaving magazines
— ideas

(actual size)

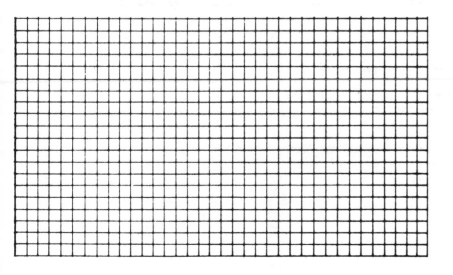

```
PATTERN -                                    REED -
PROJECT -                                    EPI  -
WARP: length     width                       SETT -
     fiber -                        TOTAL # THREADS -
WEFT: fiber -
```

sample

-notes on back-

Appendix E
Transporting Darts in Garments

It is a simple matter to change the placement of a dart from the bust to either the shoulder or neckline. Transporting darts is helpful when sewing with handwoven fabrics which do not drape particularly well because of the fabric weight, effects of the weave structure used, or shape of the person for whom the garment is being made. It is helpful to know one or two ways in which drape can be improved, particularly for the upper body. Whether the dart is transported to the shoulder or the neckline depends on the fabric, pattern line, and personal preference. Sketches by Noemi Pope.

Bust Dart to Shoulder

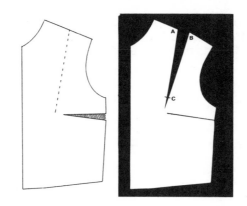

A flat pattern is shown in which the conventional bustline dart is indicated by a shaded area; the desired placement of the dart at the shoulder by a dotted line. The shoulder dart begins halfway between the neck and shoulder edges and ends just above the inner point of the bust dart and a little toward the center front.

A flat pattern in which the bust dart will be transported to the shoulder.

Close the bust dart on the flat pattern with pins, just as it would be closed on the fabric. Cut along the dotted line of the shoulder dart. Lay the pattern completely flat, opening the new shoulder dart. Add tissue paper to fill the area of the new dart. Pin the revised flat pattern to the fabric, following the instructions given with the pattern. Mark the new dart from points "A"&"B" at the shoulder edge to "C", located 1" above the original cutting line. Continue to make the garment according to the instructions.

Dart transported from the bust to the shoulder.

Bust Dart to Neck

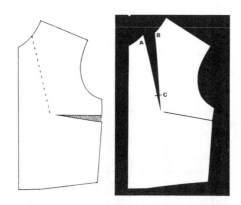

The next diagram details the transportation of a dart from the bustline to the neckline. This transportation is helpful when trying to conceal a dart. If the garment has a collar, it is possible to cover at least part of the dart with the collar.

A flat pattern in which the bust dart will be transported to the neckline.

Transport this dart using the same process as detailed for transporting the dart to the shoulder. Close the bust dart and open the neckline dart, which begins halfway between center front and the shoulder edge, and ends 1" above the inner point of the bust dart. Fill in the new dart with tissue paper and sew the dart from points "A"&"B" to "C", marked 1" above the original cutting line.

Dart transported from the bust to the neckline.

Bust and Waist to Shoulder

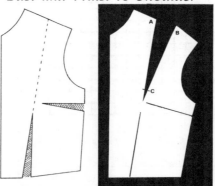

It is possible to transport two darts, the bust dart and one from the waistline, to the shoulder. This double transportation is helpful in making a jacket, blouse, or top of a dress more tailored, especially if heavier fabrics are involved.

A flat pattern in which the bust and waistline darts will both be transported to the shoulder.

Close both original darts and open the new shoulder dart, which runs from a point halfway between the shoulder and neck edges to the tip of the waistline dart. Fill in this new shoulder dart with tissue paper. Sew the dart from points "A"& "B" to "C", located at a point opposite the end of the bust dart.

Bust and waist darts transported to the shoulder.

Bibliography

Anderson, C., Gordon, J., Towner, N. *Weave Structures Used in North American Coverlets.* Olney, Maryland: Anderson, 1979.

Atwater, Mary M. *The "Spot" Weave or "Bronson" Weave.* Virginia City, Montana: The Shuttle-Craft Guild, 1948.

Atwater, Mary M. *The Summer-and-Winter Weave — Then and Now.* Virginia City, Montana: The Shuttle-Craft Guild, 1947.

Black, Mary E. *The Key to Weaving.* New York: Macmillan Publishing Co, Inc., 1980.

Burnham and Burnham, *Keep Me Warm One Night.* Toronto: University of Toronto Press, 1979.

Collingwood, Peter. *The Techniques of Rug Weaving.* New York: Watson-Guptill Publications, 1968.

Cyrus-Zetterstrom, Ulla. *Manual of Swedish Handweaving.* Newton Centre, Massachusetts: Ulla Cyrus-Zetterstrom, 1977.

Davison, Marguerite P. *A Handweaver's Pattern Book.* Chester, Pa.: Marguerite P. Davison, 1966.

Douglas, Harriet C. *Twills, Tweeds and All-Wool Fabrics.* Virginia City, Montana: The Shuttle-Craft Guild, 1949.

Douglas, Harriet C. *Interpretation of the J and R Bronson, Domestic Manufacturer's Assistant.* Virginia City, Montana: The Shuttle-Craft Guild, 1950.

Emery, Irene. *The Primary Structure of Fabrics.* Baltimore, Maryland: Textile Museum of Washington, D.C., 1980.

Gallagher, Constance D. N.. *Linen Heirlooms.* Newton Centre, Massachusetts: Gallagher, 1968.

Geijer, Agnes. *A History of Textile Art.* London: Philip Wilson Publishers Ltd., 1979.

Graves, Maitland. *The Art of Color.* New York: McGraw-Hill Book Co., 1951.

Held, Shirley E. *Weaving.* New York: Holt, Rinehart and Winston, Inc., 1973.

Itten, Johannes. *The Art of Color.* New York: Van Nostrand Reinhold Co., 1973.

Mayer, Christa C. *Masterpieces of Western Textiles.* Meriden, Connecticut: The Art Institute of Chicago, 1969.

Oelsner, G. H. *A Handbook of Weaves.* New York: Dover Publications, Inc..

Nehrer, Evelyn. *Four-Harness Huck.* New Canaan, Conn.: Evelyn Nehrer, 1953.

Regensteiner, Else. *The Art of Weaving.* New York: Van Nostrand Reinhold Company, 1972.

Rossbach, Ed. *The Art of Paisley.* New York: Van Nostrand and Reinhold Company, 1980.

Tidball, Harriet. *Double Weave, Plain and Patterned.* Lansing, Michigan: Shuttle Craft Guild, 1960.

Tidball, Harriet. *The Weaver's Book.* New York: Macmillan Publishing Co., Inc., 1974.

Zielinski, S. A. *Encyclopedia of Hand-Weaving.* Fulford, Quebec: Z-Handicrafts, 1959.

Glossary

Terms which are italicized are defined elsewhere in the glossary.

ANALOGOUS COLORS   Two colors next to one another on the *color wheel*.

BALANCED WEAVE   A weave with an equal amount of warp and weft visible on both sides of the *fabric*.

BEAM (n)   Structural part of the loom around which the warp is wound (warp beam), or woven cloth is wound (cloth beam).

BEAM THE WARP   Process by which the warp is wound onto the *warp beam*.

BLOCK WEAVE   A *fabric* involving two or more distinctly different *weave structures* which are woven simultaneously.

BROADWEFT   A term for those *freeform design techniques* involving warps sett with few ends per inch, and longer skips (or floats) in the weft.

CARTOON   A full-size drawing of a design motif which is attached to the underside of a weaving to be used as a guide when weaving.

COLOR WHEEL   A specific arrangement of the twelve colors which form the natural spectrum. This arrangement includes the *primary*, *secondary* and *tertiary colors*.

COMPLEMENTARY COLORS   Two colors opposite one another on the *color wheel*.

COUNTERBALANCE LOOM   A loom on which the activated harnesses go down.

DAMASK   A nine (or more) harness turned *twill* in which *warp- and weft-faced* twills are threaded to be woven simultaneously, each in a satin weave.

DENT   Space in a *reed*.

DENTING, CREATIVE   Altering the consecutive spacing of warp in the *reed* to create density variation.

DIRECT TIE-UPS   *Treadles* on a floor loom, or levers on a table loom, which are each *tied* to one harness.

DOUBLE WEFT   *Freeform design techniques* which are *weft-faced* on both sides of the *fabric* and require the use of two *pattern weft* yarns.

DRAPE   The flexibility of a *fabric* which determines its ability to fall in graceful folds and conform to the desired shape.

DRAW LOOM   A loom used as long ago as 4000 years on which warp threads can be lifted individually to create *sheds* for the development of surface patterns.

DRAW-DOWN   The graph of a *weave structure* which is developed according to a specific *threading*, *tie-up*, and *treadling* sequence.

EPI   Warp ends per inch.

FABRIC   The woven cloth.

FABRIC SURFACE   (See *weave surface*).

FIBER   Strands of manmade or natural material which can be spun into *yarn*.

FLOATING SELVEDGE   A single *warp end* on either side of the warp which is sleyed but is not threaded through a heddle, and provides a *plain weave selvedge*.

FREEFORM DESIGN TECHNIQUE   A system comprised of one *threading sequence* which is repeated *selvedge-to-selvedge*, and which can be *treadled* to produce at least two different *weave structures* in the same row by using separate *harness combinations* for each of the weaves.

FULLING   A finishing process for wool fabric which removes oils and fluffs the wool *fibers*.

GOLDEN MEAN   A proportionate ratio of 1:1.6 which occurs in nature and can be used in weaving to create appropriate ratios of color, design areas and dimensions.

GROUND WEFT   Rows woven in *plain weave*, which use a yarn the color and size of the warp, and follow the rows of *pattern weft* yarn, forming a firm foundation for the pattern.

HAND OF FABRIC   The feel of the *fabric* as to its drape and softness.

HARNESS COMBINATION   The harnesses lifted at one time to form a *shed* on a *rising shed loom*.

HUE   A color with specific characteristics and a designated name (red, blue, etc).

IDEA BOOK   A collection of designs, photographs, postcards, sketches, and pictures from calendars, magazines, needlepoint pattern books etc., which provide inspiration.

JACK LOOM   (See *rising shed*).

JACQUARD LOOM   A loom invented in 1803 by M. Jacquard which permitted faster weaving of intricately patterned *fabrics* than the *draw loom* by substituting punched cards for the draws.

MONOCHROMATIC COLORS   Two or more shades of one color.

MULTIPLE TIE-UPS   A floor loom on which one *harness combination* is tied to each *treadle*.

PATTERN WEFT   The weft yarn (or yarns) which form the design.

PLAIN WEAVE   A *balanced weave* in which warp and weft pass over and under one thread at a time.

PRIMARY COLOR   The three colors, red, blue, and yellow, to which no other color has been added in their formation, and from which all other colors are made.

REED   Comblike structure through which *warp ends* are threaded to keep the warp spaced evenly at the desired number of ends per inch.

RISING SHED   Loom on which the activated harnesses go up.

SECONDARY COLOR   A color formed by combining two *primary colors*.

SELVEDGE   The edges of the woven cloth.

SELVEDGE-TO-SELVEDGE   Weaving from one *selvedge* to the other.

SETT   The number of *warp ends* which are *sleyed* through each dent of the *reed*.

SETT TO SQUARE   A *fabric* woven with as many rows per inch as warp ends per inch.

SHED   The separation of warp through which the shuttle passes to form *fabric*.

SHOT   One weft row.

SHUTTLE   A device on which weft yarns are wound in order to provide easy passage of weft yarns through the *shed*. The boat shuttle houses a bobbin on which yarn is wound, whereas yarns are wound directly onto a stick shuttle.

SLEY   The process of threading *warp ends* through the *dent* in the *reed*.

TABBY   (See *plain weave*).

TERTIARY COLOR   A color formed by combining a *primary* and adjacent *secondary color*.

THREADING SEQUENCE   A specific order of harnesses which is followed in the threading and is repeated *selvedge-to-selvedge*.

THROW   The act of passing the shuttle *selvedge-to-selvedge* through the *shed*.

TIE-DOWN THREADS   Threads in the warp and/or weft which prevent long floats from occuring in the *fabric*.

TIE-UP (v)   The act of connecting the harnesses to the *treadles*.

TIE-UPS   That part of the *draw-down* indicating which harness is tied to which *treadle*.

TREADLE (v)   To activate a *harness combination*.

TREADLE (n)   A peddle on a floor loom to which cords are secured from selected harnesses in order to form *direct* or *multiple tie-ups*.

TREADLED "AS-DRAWN-IN"   A method of *treadling* in which a *harness combination* is assigned to each harness or harnesses, and *treadling* follows the *threading sequence*. The two methods of treadling as-drawn-in follow either the threading blocks or individual warp threads.

TREADLING SEQUENCE   A particular order in which the *harness combinations* are *treadled*.

TROMP AS WRIT   (See *treadled as-drawn-in*).

TWILL   A *weave structure* in which warp and weft threads pass over and under more than one thread, with the progression of rows forming a diagonal.

VALUE   The lightness or darkness of a color, according to a scale which ranges from black to white.

WARP END   An individual warp thread.

WARP-FACED   More warp shows on the *weave surface* than weft.

WEAVE STRUCTURE   The particular way in which warp and weft interact to form a specific interlacement.

WEAVE SURFACE   The upper surface of the *fabric*, which is seen by the weaver as the weaving progresses.

WEFT INLAY YARNS   Yarns which are added with the *pattern weft* to enhance a design.

WEFT-FACED   More weft shows on the *weave surface* than warp.

YARN   A strand formed by twisting *fibers* together.

Insights Index — By Chapter

Photo by John B. Searles

About The Author

Nancy Searles is a native of Buffalo, New York. She is a second generation weaver who came by her knowledge of weaving through apprenticeship within her family. She did her undergraduate studies at Skidmore College and received a graduate degree in Occupational Therapy from Tufts-Boston School of Occupational Therapy.

It was when Nancy and her family moved to Indiana in 1971 that she decided to devote full time to her two major interests, weaving and teaching. She has studied with a number of well-known fiber artists since that time, expanded her knowledge to include draw loom techniques, and has taught beginning to advanced weaving in the Art Department at Valparaiso University for the past eleven years.

During this time, Nancy has also given lectures and workshops on a broad spectrum of fiber-related topics to a steadily growing number of weaving guilds and conferences throughout the country. Articles have been published in several weaving journals covering a broad range of topics.

It was also ten years ago that Nancy began to study the weave structures inherent in block weaves and to develop the techniques of freeform design presented in this book. *The Technique of Freeform Design* is the culmination of the past ten years' research.

Index

The numbers in *italics* indicate that the topic appears in the *INSIGHTS* column.

"The best service a book can render you is, not to impart truth, but to make you think it out for yourself."

Elbert Hubbard